WHY HERMENEUTICS?

WHY HERMENEUTICS?

An Appeal Culminating with Ricoeur

ANTHONY C. THISELTON

CASCADE *Books* · Eugene, Oregon

WHY HERMENEUTICS?
An Appeal Culminating with Ricoeur

Cascade Books
An Imprint of Wipf and Stock Publishers
199 W. 8th Ave., Suite 3
Eugene, OR 97401

www.wipfandstock.com

PAPERBACK ISBN: 978-1-5326-6435-9
HARDCOVER ISBN: 978-1-5326-6436-6
EBOOK ISBN: 978-1-5326-6437-3

Cataloguing-in-Publication data:

Names: Thiselton, Anthony C., author.

Title: Why hermeneutics? : an appeal culminating with Ricoeur / Anthony C. Thiselton.

Description: Eugene, OR: Cascade Books, 2019 | Includes bibliographical references and index.

Identifiers: ISBN 978-1-5326-6435-9 (paperback) | ISBN 978-1-5326-6436-6 (hardcover) | ISBN 978-1-5326-6437-3 (ebook)

Subjects: LCSH: Hermeneutics | Bible—Hermeneutics | Hermeneutics—Religious aspects—Christianity | Ricoeur, Paul | Ricoeur, Paul—Criticism and interpretation.

Classification: BD241 T44 2019 (paperback) | BD241 (ebook)

Manufactured in the U.S.A.   11/07/19

Contents

Preface

A SEVENTH BOOK ON hermeneutics demands an explanation and defence. So far I have avoided repeating parts of earlier books, at least in the larger books of about 500 pages or more. My smaller book *Hermeneutics: An Introduction* may be the exception in part, because it was designed as a textbook. The present book aims to avoid repetition, especially in its climax on Paul Ricoeur, whose work I greatly admire.

The appeal for the essential relevance of hermeneutics has so far been only partly successful within the academy and the public arena. My teaching the subject in universities for forty years ceased only when budgetary constraints called a halt to a subject that was no longer regarded as compulsory for single honours candidates in theology. So it is worth having a final attempt at appealing for the need for hermeneutics.

As Emilio Betti observes, it ought to constitute an obligatory subject for most degree courses in the Humanities. Hermeneutics, he insists, teaches patience, tolerance, respect for other views, understanding, and humility, while holding one's own views with firmness and generosity. One of the few encouragements has been to see how the subject now features even in a number of secondary schools (for pupils aged eleven to sixteen) or sixth-form colleges (for students aged sixteen to eighteen) in the face of problems and opportunities brought by religious pluralism.

This brief study contains four chapters and a glossary. The first chapter sets out an appeal for the relevance of hermeneutics,

together with counter-arguments against this appeal. It also seeks
to explain the reasons why such a clash of convictions has emerged.
Some have commitments that underline the need for hermeneutics, but that are not shared by others. The second chapter considers
more sophisticated examples of hermeneutical practice, including
Betti, Habermas, and Gadamer. This chapter should theoretically
have included Ricoeur, but we have reserved our fourth chapter
exclusively to his work. The third chapter insists that we cannot
simply generalize about hermeneutics and texts, without specify-
ing what *kind* of text and what *kind* or reader is in view. As I argued in *New Horizons in Hermeneutics*, we must match models of
interpretation to the particular genre and the purpose of each text.
We certainly cannot generalize about hermeneutics and the Bible,
as if the Bible were a monochrome landscape. In chapter 4, I trace
thirteen insights or relatively distinctive principles in Ricoeur that
serve as a climax to my appeal for the need for hermeneutics. I
endorse these insights in my own work and commend Ricoeur for
his creative insights.

Once again I am heavily indebted to Rev. Stuart Dyas, not
only for meticulous proofreading but also for suggesting a glossary
of those terms that have a technical use in hermeneutics. The
glossary has been expanded to include fifty technical terms. Stuart
Dyas has always helped me to bear in mind possible difficulties for
the nonprofessional readers.

I am also deeply grateful to Dr. Robin Parry, editor, for
numerous improvements in clarity and style.

Anthony C. Thiselton
Emeritus Professor of Christian Theology, in the University of
Nottingham and also the University of Chester, UK
July 2019

Chapter 1

The Case for
and against Hermeneutics

1. The Universal Relevance of Hermeneutics and the Case against This

FOR NEARLY TWENTY CENTURIES the practice of hermeneutics was largely confined to the interpretation of the Bible and to the interpretation of ancient Greek poetry and literature. Although, later poetry and literature also raised and included hermeneutical problems. From the twenty-first century, however, hermeneutics became extended to other areas. In academic terms, this has been partly due to the spread of pluralism and postmodern notions. At a more popular level, it is also because many articles and newspaper reports speak of *"taking"* a report, message, or story to mean *whatever people want it to mean*. It is as if everything has tended to become entirely a matter of personal, subjective interpretation. Those who favor this approach may well speak of "the democratization of hermeneutics," or the de-privileging of the tyranny of elite specialists in the subject.

It is as if reader-response hermeneutics has moved the focus of interpretation *entirely* from the text to readers, and as if there are no limits to what a text may be said legitimately to communicate. Is everything really how we choose to "take" it? This is one of the most persistent questions in hermeneutics, which has now become extended into cultural studies. It is as if my Chester Inaugural Lecture *Can the Bible Mean Whatever We Want It to Mean?* (2005) now applies to almost everything in a very wide range of literature.[1]

The distinction between historical, legal, and theological or biblical hermeneutics on one side and literary or poetic texts on the other side has now become a huge chasm. Claims are often made for purely literary or fictional texts that few traditional biblical or theological thinkers could readily accept as applicable to Holy Scripture. Certainly the role of the reader is important, and reader-response theories of interpretation have shed much light on communication. Nevertheless, reader-response theories of a radical or extreme nature remain plausible mainly to those who hold no particular commitment to Scripture. To be more exact, the argument of chapter 3, below, is that very much depends on the particular *type* of text in view. Sometimes a given belief-system relates to the text under consideration. When some Christians approach the Bible, they may commit themselves (even tacitly) to a *covenant of* obedience and direction to the one who, they believe, speaks to them through the biblical text. They come to the text as readers who are already committed to listening and being directed. When they approach a biblical text, they do not wish to hear only themselves or their own opinions bounced back from the text.

This gives a new twist to historic debates about "the authority of the biblical text." These often became akin to technical discussions of "theories of biblical inspiration and authority."[2] A broader approach would consider whether some people take an implicitly or tacitly covenantal stance in which they pledge themselves to take seriously the standpoint of the text and the one who stands behind

---

1. Thiselton, *Can the Bible Mean Whatever We Want It to Mean?*

2. Cf. Burtchaell, *Catholic Theories of Biblical Inspiration since 1810*; Rogers and McKim, *Authority and Inspiration of the Bible*; Woodbridge, *Biblical Inspiration and Authority*.

the text. If this tacit stance is absent, however, reader-response approaches may seem to need qualification or caution. In some extreme versions of reader-response theories, "truth" becomes local, ethnocentric, and pragmatic.[3] Critics would say "relativist" and "pluralist." This is not to suggest that such theories can never have a legitimate place. Once again, it all depends on what type of text is under consideration, and what the reader's commitments and beliefs are. In the absence of firm commitments and beliefs, and in the case of purely literary or poetic texts, the appeal for the relevance of hermeneutics is not strong. We shall see that Rorty, Fish, and Lyotard do not have these constraining factors to take into account. Our question is whether their approach applies to *all* kinds of texts and to *all* kinds of readers.

2. The Undermining of Traditional Hermeneutics: Rorty, Fish, and Lyotard.

Richard M. Rorty (1931–2007) was born in New York and studied in the University of Chicago and at Yale. His position is transparent. In his introduction to his book, *Truth and Progress,* he writes, "Nobody should even try to specify the nature of truth. . . . Davidson has helped us realize *that the very absoluteness of truth is a good reason for thinking 'true' indefinable and for thinking that no theory of the nature of truth is possible. . . .* There is no truth."[4] He adds, "As long as we try to project from the relative and conditioned to the absolute and unconditioned, we shall keep the pendulum swinging between dogmatism and skepticism."[5] He writes that we "can perfectly well agree with Goodman, Putnam, and Kuhn that there is . . . No Way the World Is" (his capitals).[6] He quotes William James as saying, "'This is true' . . . just as 'the right,'

---

3. Rorty, *The Consequences of Pragmatism*; Rorty, *Contingency, Irony, and Solidarity*; Rorty, *Objectivism, Relativism, and Truth*; Rorty, *Truth and Progress*; and Rorty, *Philosophy as Cultural Politics*.

4. Rorty, *Truth and Progress*, 3 (Rorty's italics).

5. Rorty, *Truth and Progress*, 4.

6. Rorty, *Truth and Progress*, 25.

is only the expedient in the way of our behaving."[7] Put starkly, he does not believe in truth in the traditional sense. This is no surprise for those who are uncommitted to any system of truth.

Rorty is certainly not alone in his skepticism about traditional notions of truth. Although many reader-response theorists held moderate views (for example, Wolfgang Iser and Umberto Eco), Stanley Fish (b. 1938) might also be called a social pragmatist with a postmodern mind. Especially in his volume *Doing What Comes Naturally* (1989) he insists that texts cannot transform readers "from outside." In his essay "Going Down the Anti-Formalist Road" Fish observes, "Once you start down the anti-formalist road, there is no place to stop." In other words, as soon as we grasp the pragmatic relativity of criteria of meaning to social presupposition, "The general conclusion that follows is that the model in which a practice is altered or reformed by constraints brought in from the outside never in fact operates. . . . Theory has no consequences."[8] His earlier works *Self-Consuming Artifacts: The Experience of Seventeenth-Century Literature* (1972) and *Is There a Text in This Class? The Authority of Interpretative Communities* (1980) prepare the way for this conclusion, which is close to Rorty's. Both dismiss the "truth" of traditional metaphysics and hermeneutics.

Fish is just as transparent as Rorty. Textual meanings, he declares, "do not lie innocently in the world; rather, they are themselves constituted by an interpretive act. The facts one points to are still there (in a sense that would not be consoling to an objectivist) but only as a consequence of the interpretive [human-made] model that has called them to being."[9] It is justifiable, he urges, to substitute for "What does this *mean?*" the better "What does this *do?*" He writes, "The reader's response is not *to* the meaning; it *is* the meaning."[10] He further asserts, "Everything depends [on] social and institutional circumstances."[11] Rorty might have been simply

---

7. Rorty, *Truth and Progress*, 21

8. Fish, *Doing What Comes Naturally*, 2 and 14.

9. Fish, *Is There a Text in this Class*, 13.

10. Fish, *Is There a Text in this Class*, 3.

11. Fish, *Is There a Text in this Class*, 371.

reproducing Fish, except that since at least 1979 he was advocating a severely anti-representational philosophy in his *Philosophy and the Mirror of Nature.*

Fish notoriously attacks more moderate reader-response theorists, including Wolfgang Iser and Owen Fiss (especially Fiss's essay "Objectivity and Interpretation"). He even argues that Ronald Dworkin "repeatedly falls away from his own best insights into the fallacies [of pure objectivity and pure subjectivity] he so forcefully challenges."[12] In his brief allusions to Rorty he agrees with him that Rorty's polemic has no consequence, not even philosophically. More important, any consequence is "contingent upon the (rhetorical) role theory plays in the particular circumstances of a historical moment."[13]

It is not only American postmodernists who in effect threaten to destroy traditional hermeneutics. The French postmodernist Jean-François Lyotard (1924–98) published *The Differend* in 1990 in which he claimed that it is impossible to arbitrate rationally between two opposing views. They are, he alleges, "incommensurable." Rhetoric, he stated, will always enable the stronger to win over the weaker. To mark his acceptance of radical pluralism he welcomed the term "pagan" as signifying a plurality of religions. Some would argue that he presses the pluralism of the postmodernist Michel Foucault (1926–84) and others to its ultimate conclusion.

The widespread perception of Lyotard is of a thinker who saw postmodernism as protesting against the notion of one or more "grand narratives" that supposedly explained reality in terms of stories. In *The Postmodern Condition* he defined the movement as expressing "incredulity towards metanarratives," i.e., toward "universalizing" narratives such as Marx and Freud postulated to explain life.[14] In his book *The Postmodern Explained to Children*, he defines postmodernity as "war on totality."[15] He rejects all unifying structures. In politics, for example, he rejects any

---

12. Fish, *Doing What Comes Naturally*, 88

13. Fish, *Doing What Comes Naturally*, 28

14. Lyotard, *Postmodern Condition*, xxiv.

15. Lyotard, *Postmodern Explained to Children*, 24 and 31.

systematic governmental planning as "terror." Honi Fern Haber explains: "Lyotard's equation of consensus, commensurability, unity, homology, and efficiency with terror . . . is at least understandable, if not necessarily defensible, once we recognize that his understanding of language and the self . . . commits him to defend what he calls 'the pagan ideal,' . . . which amounts to radical pluralism."[16] A major difference from Rorty, of course, is his left-wing extremism compared with Rorty's touching faith in military force, tanks and guns, Western capitalism, and so-called liberal democracy. In Rorty's system or philosophy these are profoundly atheistic or godless forces.

Bill Readings defines Lyotard's use of "pagan" as "a mode of action characterized by the impiety of proceeding without criteria, making a series of site-specific little narratives that work as ruses rather than the embodiment of overarching rules."[17] Further, the impasse that Lyotard attacks but that also bedevils his work, comes to light most starkly in his book *The Differend*. Here he considers opposing parties who face each other in confrontation. Too often, he argues, the opposed views find expression through the linguistic idiom of one side only, to the exclusion of any genuine understanding of the other. Thus one side in the opposition, through the use of rhetoric, controls the discourse and thus also controls the other side. Lyotard believes that rhetoric dictates "the rules of the game," and that therefore there is no "neutral" arbiter to which one of the two sides can appeal. "The differend" (Lyotard's term) is the problem of opposed views that can neither be arbitrated or reconciled. As we shall see, this approach destroys the hermeneutical dialogue such as is urgently commended by Betti, Gadamer, and Ricoeur. As the sociologist Zygmunt Bauman points out, to deconstruct a system exhaustively into social or rhetorical convention may, indeed probably will, bring chaos.[18] Genuine debate, Lyotard claims, is no more than a device to browbeat a weaker party to conform to the rules and language imposed by the stronger party.

16. Haber, *Beyond Postmodern Politics*, 15.
17. Readings, *Introducing Lyotard*, xxxiii.
18. Bauman, *Intimations of Postmodernity*, 38.

His claim excludes rationality from hermeneutics and has the same effect on traditional interpretation as Rorty and Fish. While Rorty regards hermeneutics as no more than "a way of coping," Lyotard argues that "knowledge" is little more than a rhetorical device. Like Jean Braudillard, he sees language and knowledge as a commodity. He writes, "Knowledge in the form of an institutional commodity indispensable to productive power is already . . . the major stake in the world-wide competition for power."[19] I have developed further considerations on this approach elsewhere.[20]

3. The Traditional Search for a "Right" Meaning and a First Hint of Perspectivalism

To many in the 1980s or even 1990s, and certainly in the nineteenth century, such an approach seemed radical and relativistic, even perhaps atheistic. But Rorty dislikes and rejects the term "relativist," preferring the term "ethnocentric." In a pluralistic society this is often welcome. But "hermeneutics" can no longer mean seeking the "true" interpretation of a text. Rorty defines hermeneutics simply as a way of *coping*. He and other postmodernists would see the older, traditional aim of seeking the "right" meaning of texts as stemming from theorists like Matthias Flacius Illyricus, whose *Clavis Scripturae Sacrae* (1567) used the Aristotelian rhetorical tradition to understand the "right" meaning of the Bible. J. C. Dannhauer introduced the term "hermeneutics" to replace "interpretation" in 1654. Johannes von Felde also sought principles of interpretation that would be valid for all legal texts in his *Treatise on the Science of Interpretation* in 1689. The "purpose" and intention of the lawgiver (the author) remained a key given. In the eighteenth century the philosopher Christian Wolff also followed this tradition with its focus on authorial intention.

A move toward a *potentially* more relativist hermeneutics came in principle with Johann Martin Chladenius (1710–59). He

19. Lyotard, *Postmodern Condition*, 5
20. Thiselton, *Thiselton on Hermeneutics*, 670–75.

worked in philosophy, history, theology, and rhetoric. On the more traditional side he wrote his *Introduction to the Correct Interpretation of Reasonable Discourses and Books* (1742). Hermeneutics, he said, sought perfect or complete understanding of utterances.[21]

On the other side, however, the major insight of Chladenius was to underline the importance of "perspective" or viewpoint (*Sehe-Punkt*), which lay at the center of his historical method. Where historians left two differing accounts, this was not necessarily a contradiction. The current historical writer needs to place himself or herself into the perspective of the writer in question. Chladenius claims to find this notion of perspective or viewpoint in Leibniz's *Optics*. It can also be found in Leibniz's *Monadology*. Each historical account reflects a different perspective on the subject or event in question. According to Mueller-Vollmer, Chladenius did not perceive what radical consequences would follow. Mueller-Vollmer writes, "Any suggestion of a relativity of meanings and of interpretations was far removed from Chladenius's mind."[22] "Interpretation," Chladenius said, is nothing other than teaching someone the concepts that are necessary to learn to understand or to fully understand a speech or written work. It is not necessary to affirm that the more relativist side must lead to the skepticism of Nietzsche. Dostoyevsky and Bakhtin, as we shall see, rejected simple monologic hermeneutics without relapsing into skepticism. Meanwhile in the eighteenth century many attempted to write works on hermeneutics, of whom the most notable were perhaps J. A. Turretini of Geneva in 1728, and J. A. Ernesti of Leipzig in 1762.

4. A Major Turning-Point: Schleiermacher

The major turning-point in the history of hermeneutics came with Friedrich D. E. Schleiermacher (1768–1834). He trained as a classical philologist, originally with an interest in Plato. But from about

21. Cf. Mueller-Vollmer (ed.), *The Hermeneutics Reader*, 5–6.
22. Mueller-Vollmer (ed.), *The Hermeneutics Reader*, 7.

the age of twenty-eight to the age of thirty-four he became heavily influenced by Romanticist thinkers, especially Friedrich Schlegel, with whom he shared rooms in Berlin. The Romanticist emphasis was on life and creativity. Schleiermacher's hermeneutical goal was to relive and rethink the thoughts and feelings of the author. He no longer saw hermeneutics as a pedestrian instrumental discipline, i.e., one that served the interests of another project, or as a pedagogical subject. Hermeneutics aimed simply at *understanding* as such. Earlier even than this indebtedness to Romanticism he admired much in Kant. From him he perceived hermeneutics to be a *transcendental* discipline. It enquired into the very *basis* and *possibility* of human understanding. Hermeneutics was not simply some kind of checking procedure but involved creativity. "In interpretation, it is essential that one be able to step out of one's own frame of mind into that of another."[23] This statement belongs to the early aphorisms before 1805. The interpreter, he says, must "transform himself, so to speak, into the author."[24] Although he was primarily a New Testament scholar, he rightly saw the universal range of hermeneutics. He wrote, "Hermeneutics is part of the art of thinking."[25]

Schleiermacher also developed the principle of the hermeneutical circle, which he first found in Friedrich Ast, a roughly contemporary writer on hermeneutics. He writes, "The hermeneutical principle which Ast has proposed and in several respects developed quite extensively, is that just as the whole is understood from the parts, so the parts can be understood only from the whole. This principle is of such consequence for hermeneutics and so incontestable that one cannot even begin to interpret without using it."[26] Since that time the principle has been affirmed and used by Dilthey, Heidegger, Bultmann, Gadamer, and others. An interpreter begins to understand a text by scrutinising and examining

---

23. Schleiermacher, *Hermeneutics*, 42.
24. Schleiermacher, *Hermeneutics*, 150.
25. Schleiermacher, *Hermeneutics*, 97.
26. Schleiermacher, *Hermeneutics*, 195–96.

its parts in detail but only when an understanding of the whole is reached can interpretation seriously begin to take place.

Bultmann illustrates this from texts of mathematics and music. Unless one has an initial understanding of mathematics or music, interpretation can hardly begin; but only when the interpreter has come to appreciate the whole can interpretation be virtually complete. Rorty would presumably see this preliminary understanding as fragmented and pluriform across the varied verdicts of a liberal democracy.

As Paul Ricoeur would do later, Schleiermacher emphasized the communal aspect of hermeneutics. He writes, "The art of speaking and the art of understanding stand in relation to each other, speaking being only the outer side of thinking. . . . Speaking is the medium for the communal thought. . . . Every act of speaking is related to both the totality of the language and the totality of the speaker's thoughts."[27] In this respect the scope of hermeneutics is almost limitless, and Schleiermacher was right to stress this. Hermeneutics is much more than a way of coping (contra Rorty), it is something more fundamental.

Schleiermacher also stresses that the *effects* of a communication belong equally to hermeneutics. He writes, "The idea of the work can be understood only by the joint consideration of two factors: the *content* of the text and the range of *effects*."[28] The notion of a lone interpreter giving privilege to a text is not Schleiermacher's concern.

Schleiermacher further proposed to use contrasting methods that linked or established bridges between readers and a text. One method he called the "grammatical"; this depended on observing the rules and features of shared language. The other he called the "psychological" method; this depended on specific uses of language and also on an intuitive or psychological relation between readers and the text or its source. Certain texts demanded a recognition of their fixed status. For example, in the case of the New Testament, he argued, "Only historical interpretation can do justice

27. Schleiermacher, *Hermeneutics*, 97–98.

28. Schleiermacher, *Hermeneutics*, 151 (my italics).

to the rootedness of the New Testament authors in this time and place."[29] Each New Testament text, he says, "was addressed to specific people, and their writings could not be properly understood in the future unless these first readers could understand them."[30] This depends on the comparative method, which especially concerns systems of language.

Schleiermacher distinguishes between the psychological and grammatical methods of interpretation. The psychological method concerns human persons and their expressions of thought. Schleiermacher insists that this method involves intuitive or more-than-rational understanding. It concerns expression of a particular speaker and is entirely complementary to the comparative method of the principles of language. He argues that the grammatical and psychological methods are completely equal. Nevertheless, one method may seem "higher" *from a specific viewpoint.* He writes, "Psychological interpretation is higher when one regards the language exclusively as a means by which a person communicates his thoughts. . . . Grammatical interpretation and language . . . are higher only when one regards the person and his speaking as occasions for the language to reveal itself."[31] Like Saussure, Schleiermacher distinguishes between language as a passive system (*la langue*) and speech acts, which are dynamic (*la parole*). Wittgenstein similarly distinguishes between language and its use in life.

This all relates to what Schleiermacher regards as masculine and feminine methods in hermeneutics. The "feminine" role, he insists, involves an intuitive rapport between persons and is "divinatory"; the "masculine" method is logical and rational. The feminine is in no way "lower"; rather, each approach complements the other. He says, "Divinatory knowledge is the feminine strength in knowing people: comparative knowledge, the masculine."[32] To "divine," he says, without the comparative or philological method risks becoming a hermeneutical "nebulist"; while to engage in

29. Schleiermacher, *Hermeneutics*, 55 and 104.

30. Schleiermacher, *Hermeneutics*, 107.

31. Schleiermacher, *Hermeneutics*, 97–98.

32. Schleiermacher, *Hermeneutics*, 150.

WHY HERMENEUTICS?

linguistic and rational issues without a perception of the spirit of the subject-matter risks hermeneutical "pedantry."[33]

Schleiermacher also insists that in the light of these varied and multiple methods it would be possible for readers to understand a text "even better than its author."[34] In what sense this is true may depend on what we mean by "better." This does show that Schleiermacher never envisaged a merely wooden or literalistic repetition of the text. It is no surprise that Ernst von Dobschütz of Halle (1870–1934), in his article "Interpretation," called Schleiermacher "the pioneer of a fresh movement."[35] Rorty and Fish seem to dismiss all this elaborate hermeneutical endeavor to which the twentieth century is heir, but their minds inhabit a different universe of discourse.

Nineteenth-century writers continued in the established tradition, including H. Olshausen and H. A. W. Meyer, but not until Wilhelm Dilthey was the endeavor of Schleiermacher more fully appreciated and applied. As Dobschütz comments, hermeneutics "built upon a theory of comprehension," seeking to explain "why a given work is to be understood in one way and not in another."[36] This goal applied especially to legal texts, where, in the words of C. F. G. Heinrici, "Hermeneutics sought to make good the intention of the lawgiver."

33. Schleiermacher, *Hermeneutics*, 205.
34. Schleiermacher, *Hermeneutics*, 112.
35. Dobschütz, "Interpretation," 392; cf. 390–95.
36. Dobschütz, "Interpretation," 392.

Chapter 2

More Sophisticated Contributions to the Case

1. Wilhelm Dilthey and the Development of Sociology

WILHELM DILTHEY (1833–1911) APPLIED hermeneutics to human life and social institutions, not simply to texts. He was an admirer and biographer of Schleiermacher, although some critics lament that he has colored our view of the earlier thinker. Dilthey was educated in the Universities of Heidelberg and Berlin, reading philosophy, theology, and history. He became a professor at Basel and then Berlin, where he wrote prolifically, his complete writings running to twenty-six volumes in German, with relatively few translated into English.[1]

Dilthey's ambition was to make hermeneutics the basis of the humanities and social sciences (the *Geisteswissenschaften*). H. P. Rickman and others include Dilthey in a broadly Romanticist tradition because of his high evaluation of life and experience rather

---

1. Dilthey, *Gesammelte Schriften*, especially vols. 5 and 7 on hermeneutics. Cf. Makreel and Rodi (eds.), *Wilhelm Dilthey: Selected Works* (vol. 1, 1969, and others projected); and Dilthey, "Rise of Hermeneutics."

than thought alone.[2] H. A. Hodges speaks of his "appreciative understanding of the meaning and value of the unique individual."[3] But Dilthey's greatest interest was in social institutions—for example, in laws and codifications in communal society, being the first to apply hermeneutics to the social sciences, thus paving the way for Max Weber, Karl Mannheim, Talcott Parsons, Jürgen Habermas, Alfred Schutz, and others.

Dilthey rejects the positivism of Auguste Comte (the view that true knowledge can only derive from sense experience interpreted through reason) as naïve. (Dilthey also rejected the evolutionary ethics of Spencer on the ground that it too owed too much to empiricism.) But he followed those historians who saw the study of history as *historically conditioned*.

Before Dilthey many were influenced by Hegel's emphasis on "spirit" (*Geist*). Dilthey believed that "spirit" was too cerebral and substituted the concept and word "life" (*Leben*) in contrast to Hegel. In effect, he replaced Hegel's *Geist* (spirit) with *Leben* (life) or lived experience (*Erlebnis*). He argued, "In the veins of the knowing subject, *no real blood flows*."[4] This aphorism was aimed at Descartes and others such as Locke, Hume, and Kant, for being too artificially cerebral. A living human being is more than an abstract mind, he argued.

At the same time, there is a nexus or "connectedness (*Zuzammenhang*) between people, he said, that interweaves or binds together separate individuals. In Dilthey's view, language and signs constituted this socially connecting nexus. (We can only speculate about how he might have viewed Rorty and Fish, and Rorty's "liberal democracy.") Dilthey was critical about the capacity of introspection to provide a hermeneutical bridge. For linguistic expressions objectify subjective experiences, i.e., make and externalize passive objects of scrutiny out of them.

Dilthey's major point is that an interpreter should "re-live" (*nacherleben*) the experiences of the other by stepping out of his

2. Rickman, *Wilhelm Dilthey: Selected Writings*, 3–4.

3. Hodges, *Philosophy of Wilhelm Dilthey*, xiv.

4. Dilthey, *Gesammelte Schriften*, 5:4.

or her own shoes and exercising "sympathy" (*Hineinversetzen*) or "transposition." Understanding "the other" requires such rapport with the other that Dilthey stated, "Understanding (*Verstehen*) is the rediscovery of the 'I' in the 'you.'"[5]

Dilthey himself regarded this connectedness as making possible a "scientific" approach, for "connectedness" hints at a systematic and therefore a "scientific" approach. Expressions of life, Dilthey believed, were quasi-objective "deposits," which could be scientifically investigated. (This is a move of which Hans-Georg Gadamer strongly disapproves, from the point of view of value-laden hermeneutics.)

In his work on historical reason Dilthey in some respects anticipated Martin Heidegger. In his "Critique of Historical Reason" he writes, "The categorical characterization of life is temporality, which forms the basis for all the others. . . . Time is there for us through the synthesizing unity of consciousness.[6] . . . The ship of our life is, as it were, carried forward on a constantly moving stream. . . . The doctrine that time is merely ideal is meaningless in human studies."[7] He reflects Schleiermacher when he writes that re-living what is past shows that understanding rests on personal talent, not merely on linguistic reproduction.[8] Again, such sophisticated recognition of historical and social contingency makes it unlikely that Dilthey would have warmed to the full-scale "explanations" of Rorty and Fish. On the contrary, he regarded hermeneutics not as a way of coping, but as a foundation for the humanities and social sciences.

Zygmunt Bauman has discussed the implications of hermeneutics for social science from Dilthey onwards in his book *Hermeneutics and Social Science* (1978). He says of Dilthey, "'Putting oneself in somebody else's place' (*Sichhineinversetzen*),

5. Dilthey, *Gesammelte Schriften*, 7:191.

6. In contrast to David Hume, Dilthey stressed the *unity* of human consciousness.

7. Dilthey, *Gesammelte Schriften*, vol. 7; Dilthey, *Critique of Historical Reason*.

8. Cf. Mueller-Vollmer, *Hermeneutics Reader*, 161.

'copying' (*Nachbilden*), 're-living' (*Nacherleben*)" are key concepts for Dilthey, which provide the basis for community and social concern.[9] These activities and concepts relate the past to the present, and the individual to humankind.[10] Bauman traces the various relations between the two disciplines from Dilthey through Marx, Weber, Talcott Parsons, Mannheim, Schultz and Luckman, and Peter Berger. Max Weber considered the hermeneutical problem focussed by Dilthey, but he attempted to establish the scientific status of social theory by restricting its agenda to the sphere of instrumental reason. At the same time, Dilthey had confronted him with the relevance of historical conditioning. Can we have, Dilthey asked, "an objective understanding of an essentially subjective reality?"[11]

Tracking the story of hermeneutics and social sciences from Dilthey, Bauman observes that the social theory of Karl Marx prepared the ground for liberation hermeneutics of the third world. Bauman comments, "Marx transformed epistemology into sociology."[12] And, as we have seen, "Weber's intellectual formation came from the German debate about historical understanding."[13] Moving further on, Mannheim concluded that "partiality, distortion, and contention are and will remain a universal feature of social knowledge, and stand in the way of understanding between various groups of society."[14] Talcott Parsons "assumes that essentially subjective human action can be understood objectively."[15] Habermas, as we shall see, rejected Weber's ploy because it split apart supposed "system" from "life-world." From the standpoint of hermeneutics and of Habermas, the subjectivities and particularities of human agents become typified by Parsons into role-responses by actors. Responses can be measured, whereas personal

9. Bauman, *Hermeneutics and Social Science*, 39.

10. Bauman, *Hermeneutics and Social Science*, 40.

11. Bauman, *Hermeneutics and Social Science*, 18.

12. Bauman, *Hermeneutics and Social Science*, 58.

13. Bauman, *Hermeneutics and Social Science*, 74.

14. Bauman, *Hermeneutics and Social Science*, 19.

15. Bauman, *Hermeneutics and Social Science*, 131.

agency includes areas that are more difficult to chart. For Schutz "meaning . . . is something to be constructed, not discovered."[16]

Karl Mannheim had taken a different path.[17] He fully recognized the problem of contextual relativism, but he overpressed it into an ethnocentric account of human rationality. Each age, culture, and social class, he urged, can be assessed or understood only with reference to its own internal norms. "Utopianism" occurs when the norms of an imagined future age are applied to the present. "Ideology" imposes past norms on the present or the future. Mannheim is often said to have laid the foundations of the sociology of knowledge. Through Schutz and Luckmann this finds expression in the well-known and popularly influential book by Berger and Luckmann called *The Social Construction of Reality: A Treatise in the Sociology of Knowledge* (1966). What people often take for granted as "reality," they argue, are "social constructions" transmitted through typifications. In other words, generalizations according to predetermined categories make it more certain that we have "constructed" what we portray as "reality." They write, "The social reality of everyday life is thus apprehended in a continuum of typifications . . . structured in terms of relevances."[18] Bauman argues that the task of hermeneutics for social science is that of "*constructing a form of life of a 'higher order' which will incorporate previous [ones] as . . . sub-forms.*"[19] This, he says, involves seeing the general in the particular "by enlarging both the alien's and one's own experience so as to construct a large system which 'makes sense' to the other."[20] Bauman follows Habermas in seeking a broader basis of intersubjectivity that forms of life can share.[21] Bauman's critical survey shows how inextricably hermeneutics and social science are bound together.

16. Bauman, *Hermeneutics and Social Science*, 181.

17. Mannheim, *Ideology and Utopia*.

18. Mannheim, *Ideology and Utopia*, 76.

19. Bauman, *Hermeneutics and Social Science*, 217 (his italics).

20. Bauman, *Hermeneutics and Social Science*, 218.

21. Bauman, *Hermeneutics and Social Science*, 240.

2. Betti and Habermas

Emilio Betti (1890–1968)

Emilio Betti was an Italian jurist and specialist in hermeneutics and Roman law, emphasizing the importance of the author's intention. Like Hegel, Dilthey, and Heidegger, he stressed the importance of situatedness-within-history, attending to Hegel's notion of process. On the other hand, he aimed at objectivity, in contrast to Hans-Georg Gadamer, the classic German writer on hermeneutics, with whom he has debated this issue. Betti valued the concepts of "open-mindedness" (*Aufgeschlossenheit*) and "receptiveness" (*Empfänglichkeit*).[22] Most important of all in relation to our concerns, he insists that hermeneutics is an intellectual discipline and educational skill that is essential and fundamental for life. Betti writes, "For humankind nothing lies so close to the heart as understanding one's fellow human beings."[23]

This process of understanding one's fellow human beings, Betti says, entails a willingness to listen with respect and patience. (This also has parallels with Christian concerns about love.) We need to listen not only to *what* has been said, but also to *why* it has been said. He even suggests that *hermeneutics should be an obligatory university subject in the humanities*. This principle, he says, "Welled up so nobly in the Romantic period as the common concern of all the humane disciplines," as seen in Humboldt, Böckh, and Dilthey.[24] Betti has made the same point in his work *Zur Grundlegung einer allgemeinen Auslegungslehre* (1955). He regrets that Heidegger's influence in Germany was such that his own concerns were not taken with full seriousness.

22. Betti, *Allgemeine Auslegungslehre als Methodik der Geisteswissenschaften*, 21; cf. 1–61.

23. Betti, *Allgemeine Auslegungslehre als Methodik der Geisteswissenschaften*, 7 (2nd ed., 1972)

24. Betti, *Allgemeine Auslegungslehre als Methodik der Geisteswissenschaften*, 6–7

In contrast to Gadamer, Betti distinguishes interpretation (*Auslegung*) from meaning-giving (*Sinngebung*), i.e., from the view that hermeneutics concerns, in Palmer's words, "the interpreter's conferring meaning on the object" to be understood.[25] This rejected view seems to be akin to the position of Rorty and Fish. However, in contrast to this, Betti, like Dilthey, seeks the objectification of the human spirit in *reconstructing the meaning and intention of an author*. Like Dilthey, Betti sees this interpretative act as an inversion of the creative process of the author. "The interpreter must penetrate the foreignness and otherness of the object"; if he or she fails, "he succeeds only in projecting his own subjectivity on the object of interpretation" (as in Rorty or Fish).[26] While there is no escape from the interpreter's own understanding in the act of interpretation, hermeneutics cannot be reduced to projecting our existing understanding onto that which we seek to understand. Such would be a solipsistic bondage to the self.

Betti even regards this bondage to the self as a potential risk in Bultmann's notion of pre-understanding. Betti writes, "The text to which the preunderstanding gives meaning is not simply there to strengthen some previously held opinion; rather, we must assume that *the text has something to say to us which we do not already know from ourselves* and which exists *independently of our act of understanding*."[27] Again, Bultmann's view of preunderstanding prematurely merges "interpretation" with *Sinngebung* or the interpreter's conferring meaning onto the text. These words might well have been written in anticipation of Rorty, Fish, and radical postmodernists. Betti even accuses Gadamer of a standardless subjectivity.

25. Palmer, *Hermeneutics*, 56.

26. Palmer, *Hermeneutics*, 57.

27. Betti, *Die Hermeneutik als allgemeinen Methodik der Geisteswissenschaften*, 35 (my italics).

Jürgen Habermas (b. 1929)

Jürgen Habermas is one of the most influential thinkers of socio-critical hermeneutics. He studied first at the University of Bonn and for five years worked as an assistant in the Institute for Social Research in Frankfurt under Theodore Adorno and Max Horkheimer. He became Professor of Philosophy and Sociology at Frankfurt in 1964. His major works include *Theory and Practice* (German, 1963; English, 1973*); Knowledge and Human Interests* (German, 1968; English, 1971); *The Theory of Communicative Action* (2 vols., German, 1982; English, 1984 and 1987); and *The Philosophical Discourse of Modernity: Twelve Essays* (German, 1985; English, 1987). This last work traces the rise of the Frankfurt School, and engages in discussion with Lyotard about postmodernism.

Against such relativism and pluralism, along with Karl-Otto Apel, Habermas remains resolute in attempting to formulate the transcendental, meta-critical, philosophical position that seeks both to affirm the critical or quasi-transcendental capacity of social theory grounded in intersubjective communicative interaction, alongside instrumental or technical reason, and also to retain some notion of the universal or trans-contextual nature of human rationality.

Habermas wrestles with the problem of offering a social critique of systems, which include positivism, post-Enlightenment rationalism, and "alterity" or "otherness." This task requires a transcendental frame (i.e., a criterion brought in from without) within which to establish the validity of the critique; but if social practice and communicative interaction play the decisive part that Habermas's social theory ascribed to them, this frame will be, in the words of Stephen White, "nonfoundational universalism" and will perhaps not even be a frame.[28] Bernstein observes this dilemma: "To speak of 'the pathology of modernity' . . . presupposes a normative standard for judging what is pathological. . . . Can we still, in our time, provide a rational justification for universal normative

28. White, *Recent Work of Jürgen Habermas*, esp. 1–68.

standards? Or are we faced with relativism, . . . which holds that ultimate norms are arbitrary?"[29] Adorno and Horkheimer wrestled with this question.

Habermas's *Knowledge and Human Interests* (1978) expounds his fundamental critique of positivist theories of knowledge, a critique that is also basic to the hermeneutical theories of Gadamer, Ricoeur, Pannenberg, and Apel. He speaks of this critique of hermeneutics as "meta-hermeneutics."[30] (The demand for metacriticism places Habermas alongside Apel.) While he endorses Gadamer's work on the nature of hermeneutical understanding, he rejects the latter's arguments about the inevitable primacy of linguistic tradition as an ontological principle. Habermas claims that there is a social consensus on which authority is founded, free from force. He further claims that there is the need for a critique of epistemology. He argues, "This radical critique of knowledge is possible only as social theory."[31] He also endorses Marx's critique of Hegel that "Labour or work is not only a fundamental category of human existence but also an epistemological category."[32] In the background stands Marx's key statement: "It is not men's consciousness that determines their existence, but on the contrary their social existence which determines their consciousness."[33] Bauman calls this principle "A programme of hermeneutics-turned-sociology."[34] This becomes the core in much liberation hermeneutics, where political situations or gender situations determine almost everything.

On the positive side, Habermas observes: "Positivism stands or falls with the principle of scientism, that is that the meaning of knowledge is defined by what sciences do."[35] In other words, knowledge serves only instrumental interests. In opposition to this approach, Dilthey would have taken intersubjectivity as his

29. Bernstein, *Habermas and Modernity*, 4; cf. 1–32.
30. Habermas, "Hermeneutic Claim to Universality," 203.
31. Habermas, *Knowledge and Human Interests*, vii.
32. Habermas, *Knowledge and Human Interests*, 28
33. Marx and Engels, *Über Kunst und Literatur*, 1:74.
34. Bauman, *Hermeneutics and Social Science*, 58.
35. Habermas, *Knowledge and Human Interests*, 67.

extended frame of reference (though not in Rorty's pragmatic sense). And Habermas would have agreed. Habermas also draws on the later Wittgenstein to show that language and action interpret each other reciprocally.

Like liberation hermeneutics, Habermas regards the exposure of "interest" (i.e., the political or social presuppositions or horizons that color our interpretation) as "emancipatory." In his discussion of Freud, he writes, "The starting point of psychoanalytical theory is the experience of . . . the blocking force that stands in the way of free and public communication of repressed contents. . . . The unconscious impulses do not want to be remembered."[36] Habermas called this critical frame "depth-hermeneutics."[37]

Habermas's work is impressive, and it should not be denied that the social dimension of all hermeneutics must be taken into account. However, is his critique genuinely transcendental? Or is it derived from a social theory that is contingent? How can engagement in a particular form of social or political struggle be identified with transcendental reflection on necessary or universal conditions of knowledge? We may also turn to the more recent two-volume work *The Theory of Communicative Action*.[38] This work argues for a "paradigm-shift" that locates "the foundations of social science in the theory of communication." He traces three roots of communicative action: the propositional, the illocutionary, and the expressive.[39] Here he points explicitly to the work of John L. Austin on performative language or speech acts, and the thought of the later Wittgenstein.[40] He stresses the subjectivity of the human speaker and addressee as agents who share a life-world shaped by shared horizons and common behavior-situations.

Nevertheless, some account must also be taken of language and social practice as a system that *transcends this context of human subjectivity*. These two aspects reflect the great methodological

36. Habermas, *Knowledge and Human Interests*, 229 and 231.
37. Habermas, *Knowledge and Human Interests*, 272.
38. Habermas, *Theory of Communicative Action*, 2:3.
39. Habermas, *Theory of Communicative Action*, 2:67.
40. Austin, *How to Do Things with Words*.

divide not only in linguistic theory but also in different traditions and modern sociology. Speech-acts and hermeneutics oppose structure and semiological theory; hermeneutical and value-orientated approaches stand in contrast to structural-functional or quasi-objectivist approaches. This becomes Habermas's key contrast *between "system" and "life-world."* He argues that the splitting apart of the "life-world" and "system" occurs in a classic form in Max Weber (1864–1920). Weber began to work with Dilthey's notion of life-world, but his sociology led him to concentrate on the supposedly value-neutral methods of quantification and statistical description, and to limit the notion of rationality to instrumental reason. Bauman argues that Weber paid too much attention to economics as a way to resolve all the tasks posited by historical understanding.[41]

Habermas opposed the ahistorical and formal rationalism of Parsons, and his "objectivism." Rather, he explores a model of linguistic and behavioral interaction. To speak a language is to perform an act, and linguistic acts depend on certain shared presuppositions. This is utterly correct. But Habermas emphasizes how these presuppositions relate to social roles (following George H. Mead). He writes, "Mead connects the concept of social role in the sense of the norm that . . . entitles group members to expect certain actions from one another in certain situations."[42] Two poles are beginning to relate to each other. On the one hand, language is a matter of action by social agents, and this approach sees everything in terms of what is *incomplete* and ongoing. On the other hand, we cannot understand or critically evaluate the interpersonal language-game as life-world without reference to *the system* that transcends it. Each pole represents a different dimension of human rationality. A "communicative" rationality may be distinguished from a "purposive" rationality.

The life-world belongs to the hermeneutical level of interpersonal understanding and cooperative behavior. It coheres with the hermeneutical nature of communication. But Habermas insists

41. Bauman, *Hermeneutics and Social Science*, 69; cf. 69–88.
42. Habermas, *Theory of Communicative Action*, 2:37.

that contextual-behavioral features are transcended in a larger system. System provides a frame or dimension for ideological or social critique. It is not simply descriptive or pragmatic. Habermas writes, "As long as they maintain a performative attitude, communicative actors cannot reckon with systematic distortion of their communication."[43] Without system, we stand under the illusion that language is transparent and conveys only its surface-meaning. We uncritically believe that agents or subjects of speech acts are entirely conscious of their motivations and the constraints that drive them. Life-world should not be reduced to system; neither should judgement be reduced to life-world.

Nevertheless, Habermas argues that there has been a progressive uncoupling of system and life-world in modernity.[44] Bureaucratic mechanisms of the state apparatus, the market economy, and laws with interests of certain sub-groups preserved at the expense of others, have all precipitated this detachment. He believes that his method of approach exposes these inhibiting factors. At this point he alludes again to Karl Marx. Marx, he argues, revealed that a capitalist commodity structure presupposes norms or laws that make "a mockery of bourgeois ideals."[45] Habermas stresses the "unmasking" character of his work as a socio-critical tool. He draws on a variety of traditions in philosophy, sociology, and linguistic theory. But his work remains a profoundly hermeneutical theory alongside the work of Dilthey, Betti, Apel, Gadamer, and Ricoeur. And as with their work, it is not like Rorty's socio-pragmatic contextualism (see glossary).

3. Hans-Georg Gadamer

Hans-Georg Gadamer (1900–2002) was born in Marburg, and educated in the University of Breslau, where he worked on literature, languages, and philosophy. In 1922–23 he began to consider

43. Habermas, *Theory of Communicative Action*, 2:150.
44. Habermas, *Theory of Communicative Action*, 2:153–97.
45. Habermas, *Theory of Communicative Action*, 2:185.

the difference for thinking between "problems" and "questions." Problems, he would later say, are fixed abstractions, like fixed stars in the sky. Questions, by contrast, perhaps like meteors, arise out of a context, and lead somewhere. In his later magisterial work *Truth and Method* (1st German ed. 1960) he wrote, "Problems are not real questions that arise of themselves, and hence acquire the pattern from the genesis of their meaning but are alternatives that can only be accepted in themselves."[46]

Also, in 1923, Gadamer came under the influence of Martin Heidegger, to whom he became a close follower, studying Schleiermacher, Dilthey, and the German hermeneutical tradition. He also worked on Aristotle and came to respect the "wisdom" (*phronesis*) of the ancient Greeks. But he was no mere clone of Heidegger. Like Heidegger in his later thought, Gadamer shared with him a passion for art and the history of art, and also stressed the importance of passive meditation (German *Gelassenheit*).

In one important respect Gadamer reversed the flow of the Enlightenment. Whereas René Descartes and his successors regarded the epistemological flow in interpretation to proceed from the active human subject to a passive text as object of scrutiny, Gadamer, in James M. Robinson's words, reversed the flow of subject and object, almost like Karl Barth.[47] He writes, "Thus the flow of the traditional relation between subject and object, in which the subject interrogates the object, and, if he masters it, obtains from it his answer, has been significantly reversed. For now it is the object—which should henceforth be called the subject matter—that puts the subject in question."[48] Like Robert Funk, Robinson makes these comments initially in relation to Karl Barth and Ernst Fuchs, but he soon reintroduces them in relation to Gadamer.[49]

For my undergraduate class in theology, this became a turning-point in their approach to the biblical writings. For

46. Gadamer, *Truth and Method*, 377.

47. Robinson, "Hermeneutic Since Barth," 53–56 and 63–65; cf. 1–77.

48. Robinson, "Hermeneutic Since Barth," 23–24

49. Funk, *Language, Hermeneutic, and Word of God*, 11–13, 42–44, and 64; and Robinson, "Hermeneutic Since Barth," 26–27.

many students it became the key point in their enthusiasm for hermeneutics. Fuchs uses the illustration of the hermeneutical moment as placing a mouse in front of a cat. This illustrates "What shows itself in this text?"[50] In the teaching of Jesus, Fuchs insists, the text "singles out the individual and grasps him deep down."[51] Further, "The text is meant to live."[52] He says, "The truth has ourselves as its object," and "The texts must translate us before we can translate them."[53]

Like Gadamer, Fuchs insists that the subject-matter comes to speech through language as a language-event (German, *Sprachereignis*). This achieves a focus in Gadamer's analogies between uses of language and games, festivals, and musical performance. Play, he writes, "fulfils its purpose only if the player loses himself in the play."[54] He explains: "*The primacy of the play over the consciousness of the player* is fundamentally acknowledged."[55]

A second inference from these analogies is that each actual performance varies in operation and cannot be predicted simply by "rules." If every football match or musical performance was utterly identical with every previous one, and the result could be predicted, there would be no point to the performance. Gadamer writes, "*All encounter with the language of art is an encounter with an unfinished event and is itself part of this event.*"[56]

We appear to have moved far away from the search for a single "right" meaning in hermeneutics. Might Rorty, Fish, and Lyotard have a point? They do have insight, but they go too far. There is no need to go to such extremes, for the choice is not between texts having either a single, fixed meaning or an infinite plurality of meanings—intermediate stances are possible. Indeed, different

50. Robinson, "Hermeneutic Since Barth," 46 and 53–54; and Fuchs, *Hermeneutik*, 109.

51. Fuchs, *Studies of the Historical Jesus*, 35.

52. Fuchs, *Studies of the Historical Jesus*, 193

53. Fuchs, "New Testament and the Hermeneutical Problem," 143.

54. Gadamer, *Truth and Method*, 102.

55. Gadamer, *Truth and Method*, 104 (Gadamer's italics).

56. Gadamer, *Truth and Method*, 99 (Gadamer's italics).

kinds of text may be more or less open to fluidity in interpretation. As J. Lotman and Umberto Eco point out, there is all the difference in the world between a "closed" text (e.g., an instruction manual) and an "open" text (e.g., a poem). Eco speaks of "engineering" or "transmissive" cultures with their "closed" texts and "literary" or multi-layered communication that is more "open." We shall explore this in chapter 3. Certainly Gadamer's analogies are correct in the case of "open" texts. However, transmissive texts arguably do still have a "right" meaning.

A further reason for Gadamer's stress on unpredictability is the decisive flow of history and historicality, or how every person and event is radically conditioned by their place in history, i.e., by their historical and social situation. He learned this most of all from Heidegger. He regards the history of philosophy as marking a great schism between the rationalism of Descartes and the Enlightenment and the more history-aware tradition of Giambattista Vico (1668–1744) and the *Geisteswissenschaften* (humanities and social sciences). He places himself emphatically in the second tradition. Hermeneutics, he says, begins "from experience of art and historical tradition."[57]

In *Truth and Method*, the word "method" is ironic, set almost in opposition to truth. The historical and more hermeneutical tradition is represented not only by Vico, but also, according to Gadamer, by the Roman sense of the communal (*sensus communis*) and by the common sense school of Scottish philosophy, as represented by Thomas Reid.[58] The qualities that this tradition offered were wisdom (*phronēsis*), the importance of application, and the relevance of the heart as well as the mind. He even appeals to the eighteenth-century pietist F. C. Oetinger to argue that clarity is not enough. He also begins to explore the *sensus plenior* (i.e., the "fuller sense" of texts beyond their immediate meaning) so beloved by mediaeval theologians and pietists. It is no accident that Gadamer introduces this near the beginning of his book. Oetinger attacked the rationalist hermeneutics of Christian Wolff.

57. Gadamer, *Truth and Method*, xxiii.
58. Gadamer, *Truth and Method*, 19–30.

As he proceeds with Part One of his book, he constantly attacks the enemy of abstraction, and extols the value of "experience" (*Erlebnis*).[59]

Gadamer heads the final section of Part One, "The Ontology of the Work of Art and Its Hermeneutical Significance." Here he introduces his controlling metaphors of games, festivals, and other kinds of performance. He first takes up the concept of play from aesthetics.[60] Play, he says, "contains its own, even sacred, seriousness."[61] The victor in a game emerges in the to-and-fro movement of the game. Each game presents the person who plays it with a task.[62] Play draws a player into these tasks, which dominate his consciousness. A child playing "is totally absorbed."[63] The game is a part of "the event of being that occurs in representation (*Darstellung*) and belongs essentially to play as play."[64]

The criterion for a correct representation is "highly flexible" and relative.[65] This also applies to festivals. Because of variations in time their identity may vary.[66] Gadamer explains, "A festival exists only in being celebrated."[67] He also uses the example of preaching, where the gospel is reinforced in the presentation.[68] "By being presented, it [the play, the festival, or the gospel] experiences, as it were, an increase in being."[69] This is seen most clearly, he observes, in the performing arts.[70] He also alludes to architecture where a work has no real "presence" without some sort of mediation.[71] In

59. Gadamer, *Truth and Method*, 35–100.

60. Gadamer, *Truth and Method*, 101.

61. Gadamer, *Truth and Method*, 102.

62. Gadamer, *Truth and Method*, 107.

63. Gadamer, *Truth and Method*, 108; cf. 109.

64. Gadamer, *Truth and Method*, 116.

65. Gadamer, *Truth and Method*, 119.

66. Gadamer, *Truth and Method*, 122–24.

67. Gadamer, *Truth and Method*, 124.

68. Gadamer, *Truth and Method*, 127.

69. Gadamer, *Truth and Method*, 140.

70. Gadamer, *Truth and Method*, 147.

71. Gadamer, *Truth and Method*, 157.

the end, he compares hermeneutics in Schleiermacher and Hegel: the former focuses on reconstruction; the latter, on integration.

This brings us to Part Two of *Truth and Method*. In the second main part Gadamer examines more deeply the questions of truth, understanding, and historical reason. He begins by reflecting on the hermeneutical circle in Schleiermacher, which was taken up by Heidegger and Bultmann. He admits that the circular relationship between whole and the parts "is not new. It was already known to classical rhetoric."[72] He then traces the pre-history of Romanticist hermeneutics. He may even give a partial recognition of "transmissive" texts, when he says, "The literal meaning of Scripture . . . is not univocally intelligible in every place and every moment," although his main point here is to underline allegorical interpretation.[73] In spite of Schleiermacher's insights, Gadamer has strong reservations about the notion of "psychological laws" in Schleiermacher's hermeneutics.[74]

Gadamer commends Wilhelm Dilthey for wrestling with questions left by G. W. F. Hegel, especially the question of historical conditionedness or situatedness, and how history transforms persons.[75] He also commends him for noting the universal scope of hermeneutics rather than viewing it as a service discipline for theology, focused on the interpretation of the Bible.[76] In passing he notes Chladenius's concept of "point of view."[77] His major interest, however, is in the historical and the concept of universal history, including the contributions of Leopold von Ranke and Johann Gustav Droysen. But most important of all is Hegel. Inspired by Hegel's complex thought, Gadamer declares, "*Thus the foundation for the study of history is hermeneutics.*"[78]

---

72. Gadamer, *Truth and Method*, 173.

73. Gadamer, *Truth and Method*, 175.

74. Gadamer, *Truth and Method*, 184–97.

75. Gadamer, *Truth and Method*, 177 and 197–99.

76. Gadamer, *Truth and Method*, 177.

77. Gadamer, *Truth and Method*, 182.

78. Gadamer, *Truth and Method*, 199 (Gadamer's italics).

After a detailed study of Ranke and Droysen, Gadamer returns to Dilthey. He values Dilthey's notion of "life-world." But if
life is the inexhaustible, creative reality that Dilthey thinks it, then
must not the constant alteration of historical context preclude any
knowledge from attaining to objectivity?[79] The transformation of
people in mutual dialogue is "the secret of all education."[80] Dilthey is still too much a child of the Enlightenment.[81] He regards
Dilthey's conclusions as too "scientific" and law-bound.[82] Next,
Gadamer advances to consider the founder of phenomenology,
Edmund Husserl. For Husserl and for most exponents of hermeneutics, the concept of "horizon" was fundamental.[83]

"Horizon" is a better word than "position" or "presupposition," since the latter imply a fixed place, whereas horizons change
and move (for example, for an observer in a train or car). And they
may expand, as in hermeneutics and in Wolfhart Pannenberg's
theology. In Gadamer's thought, the notion of horizon relates to a
flow of experience: "A horizon is not a rigid boundary but something that moves with one and invites one to advance further."[84]
He writes, "Life-world is the antithesis of all objectivism."[85] In the
end, however, "life" plays the same part as in Dilthey.

Gadamer next turns to consider a theory of hermeneutical
experience. He discusses Heidegger on historicity and the disclo-
sure of "the fore-structure of understanding." He combines this
with an overt attack on Enlightenment rationalism. He writes,
"The fundamental prejudice of the Enlightenment is the prejudice
against prejudice itself, which denies tradition its power."[86] Only
from the Enlightenment does "prejudice" take on a negative conno-
tation. He argues that self-reflection and autobiography—Dilthey's

79. Gadamer, *Truth and Method*, 231.
80. Gadamer, *Truth and Method*, 233.
81. Gadamer, *Truth and Method*, 239–41.
82. Gadamer, *Truth and Method*, 241–42.
83. Gadamer, *Truth and Method*, 245.
84. Gadamer, *Truth and Method*, 245.
85. Gadamer, *Truth and Method*, 247.
86. Gadamer, *Truth and Method*, 270.

starting points—are not primary and are therefore not an adequate basis for the hermeneutical problem. He writes, "The focus of subjectivity is a distorting mirror. The self-awareness of the individual is only a flickering in the closed circuits of historical life. *That is why the prejudices (Vorurteile) of the individual, far more than his judgements, constitute the historical reality of his being.*"[87]

Gadamer further endorses Heidegger's notion of temporality (*Zeitlichkeit*). He then argues for the rehabilitation of authority and tradition. He writes,

> The authority of persons is ultimately based not on the subjection and abdication of reason, but on an act of acknowledgement and knowledge . . . that the other is superior to oneself in judgement and insight and that for this reason judgement takes precedence–i.e. it has priority over one's own. [It] trusts to the better insight of others. Authority in this sense, properly understood, has nothing to do with blind obedience to commands. Indeed, authority is to do not with obedience but rather with knowledge.[88]

Gadamer's last main sections in this Part Two concern the history of effects (*Wirkungsgeschichte*) and an analysis of historically-effected consciousness.[89] Again, Gadamer insists, "The horizon is something to which we move and that moves with us. Horizons change for a person who is moving. Thus the horizon of the past, out of which all human life lives and which exists in the form of tradition, is always in motion."[90] He adds, "Understanding always involves something like applying a text to be understood to be with the interpreter's present situation."[91] Hegel was right, he adds, to regard the basis of hermeneutics as the mediation of history and truth.[92]

---

87. Gadamer, *Truth and Method*, 276–77 (Gadamer's italics).

88. Gadamer, *Truth and Method*, 279 (his italics).

89. Gadamer, *Truth and Method*, 300–379.

90. Gadamer, *Truth and Method*, 304.

91. Gadamer, *Truth and Method*, 308.

92. Gadamer, *Truth and Method*, 341.

The dialectic of experience has its proper fulfilment "not in definitive knowledge, but in the openness to experience that is made possible by experience itself."[93] Every experience worthy of the name thwarts an expectation: "For tradition is a genuine partner dialogue, and we belong to it, as does the I with a Thou."[94] He concludes, "Openness to the other, then, involves recognising that I myself must accept some things that are against me, even though no one else forces me to do so."[95]

This leads on to Gadamer's emphasis on the hermeneutic priority of the question. Here he draws on Plato for the priority of questioning and, in our period, R. G. Collingwood for "the logic of question and answer."[96] The logic of question and answer that Collingwood elaborated should put an end to talk about permanent "problems." Gadamer declares, "Reflection on the hermeneutical experience transforms problems back to questions that arise and that derive their sense from their motivation."[97] This brings us back to our starting-point and concludes the crucially important Part Two.

Part Three of *Truth and Method* mainly concerns language and communication, yet earlier themes continue. Gadamer writes, "Conversation is a process of coming to an understanding. Thus it belongs to every true conversation that each person opens himself to the other, truly accepts his point of view as valid and transposes himself into the other to such an extent that he understands not the particular individual but what he says."[98] The interpreter "clearly exemplifies the reciprocal relationship that exists between interpreter and text. . . . Only through him are the written marks changed back into meaning."[99] Like a conversation, "interpretation is a circle closed by the dialectic of question and

93. Gadamer, *Truth and Method*, 355.
94. Gadamer, *Truth and Method*, 358.
95. Gadamer, *Truth and Method*, 361.
96. Gadamer, *Truth and Method*, 369–79.
97. Gadamer, *Truth and Method*, 377.
98. Gadamer, *Truth and Method*, 385.
99. Gadamer, *Truth and Method*, 387.

answer. . . . Understanding (in language) *is the concretion of historically effected consciousness.*"[100]

Perhaps less relevant to our main concerns is Gadamer's assessment of the development of the concept of language in the history of Western thought, beginning with Plato. Plato's emphasis on convention rather than nature is widely accepted by most specialists in linguistics. Even Gadamer's emphasis on the Word in John's Gospel (John 1:1–18) is hardly controversial.[101] His work on concept formation is more relevant, but in general this lacks the sharpening that might have come from British linguistic philosophy. On the whole, he tends to owe more to the older German philosophy of language of Wilhelm von Humboldt than to more modern Anglo-American writers. On the other hand, he does produce insightful work on the notion of language worlds.[102] He concludes by exploring "language as a horizon of a hermeneutic ontology."[103]

We should not assume that *Truth and Method* is Gadamer's only work on hermeneutics. A six-hundred-page volume, *The Philosophy of Hans-Georg Gadamer* (1997), edited by Lewis Hahn, contains his "Reflections on My Philosophical Journey" and twenty-nine critical essays. In his autobiographical reflections Gadamer declares, "Hermeneutics is above all a practice. . . . It is the heart of all education that wants to teach how to philosophize. In it what one has to exercise is above all the ear."[104] The text and language are active; the interpreter must learn to *listen* and to *perceive*.

Although he is heavily biased towards German philosophy of language, Gadamer includes a passing reference to Ludwig Wittgenstein and his concept of "language games."[105] He adds, "When one understands what another person says, this is not

---

100. Gadamer, *Truth and Method*, 389 (his italics).

101. Gadamer, *Truth and Method*, 419–28.

102. Gadamer, *Truth and Method*, 446–56.

103. Gadamer, *Truth and Method*, 456–91.

104. Hahn, *Philosophy of Hans-Georg Gadamer*, 17.

105. Hahn, *Philosophy of Hans-Georg Gadamer*, 19.

only something meant, it is also something shared."[106] In his *Philosophical Hermeneutics* (1976) Gadamer again refers in passing to Wittgenstein.[107] More significantly, he betrays his suspicion of what passes for "facts." He writes, "What is established by statistics seems to be a language of fact, but which questions these facts answer and what facts would begin to speak if other questions were asked are hermeneutical questions."[108] We may well sympathize with this correct point, but it also adds fuel to Wolfhart Pannenberg's major criticism that Gadamer devalues facts and assertions as such.[109]

We may have reservations about Gadamer's pluralism and his lack of balance in the need to stress explanation as well as understanding (an imbalance later corrected by Ricoeur), but his emphasis on the critical role of tradition in hermeneutics and his notion of the active role of the reader or interpreter in the actualization of a text are only two of the many deep insights that have enriched the development of hermeneutics. Above all he has shown the severe limitations of the outlook of the Enlightenment and its legacy. His particular development of the analogy of "games" or "festivals" with understanding has proved to be illuminating.

This chapter has sought to show that Betti's emphasis on the obligatory nature of hermeneutics, Habermas' work on communicative action, and Gadamer's insights on hermeneutical horizons, tradition, and the active role of the reader are crucial and warrant careful attention.

---

106. Hahn, *Philosophy of Hans-Georg Gadamer*, 53.

107. Gadamer, *Philosophical Hermeneutics*, 127.

108. Gadamer, *Philosophical Hermeneutics*, 11

109. Pannenberg, *Theology and the Philosophy of Science*, 168.

Chapter 3

Different Types of Texts

Eco, Ricoeur, and Others

1. The First Stage: Open and Closed Texts; Semiotics and Umberto Eco

THE MOST BASIC AND fundamental division of types of texts is the contrast between what we might call (for want of a better term) "open" and "closed" texts. This distinction is often associated especially with Umberto Eco and his work on "codes" in semiotics (see glossary) or the theory of signs and signification, even though some writers prefer other ways of describing open or closed texts. He recognizes the need for both a theory of codes (signification) and a theory of sign-production (communication). Eco readily acknowledges that he first drew this distinction from Jurij Lotman.[1] Lotman distinguished between categories of communication: between those that function primarily to *transmit* or to communicate meanings and those that serve to *generate* or to produce meanings.

The former reflect a "handbook" or "engineering" culture, or a convention that operates with generally stable meanings. Even in

---

1. Eco, *Theory of Semiotics*, 136–37.

a handbook culture, texts may embody more than one code, and then meaning may depend on a *reader's choice* of what code he or she uses to decode a meaning. Following Lotman, Eco concludes that "re-readings" can produce changes of code, which modify the meaning of the text or work. Sometimes a "first" reader may use a different code with its consequent meaning from a "second" reader. Lotman's working contrast forms part of the foundation of Eco's work in *The Role of the Reader* (1981) and his *Semiotics and the Philosophy of Language* (1984), as well as his earlier work *A Theory of Semiotics* (1976). In *Semiotics and the Philosophy of Language* Eco distinguishes between "communication signs" (e.g., emblems, street signs, or trademarks) and "premonitory signs" (e.g., metaphors, traces, or ancient ruins). The former (signs, etc.) presuppose matching codes; the latter (metaphors, etc.) incorporate multiple interpretations.

In theory, "premonitory signs" can expand into an outward-moving, growing, labyrinth. Gadamer stressed this possibility, but we noted that it was a problem that he did not seem to take account of transmissive texts in his theory of hermeneutics and language. Even if we take full account of the history and historicity of language uses, there is nevertheless the possibility of *transient revaluations* of language uses (i.e. ones that relate only to temporary uses of language).

Linguists rightly stress the synchronic as well as the diachronic dimension of language. On this basis Eco attempts to outline a theory of codes that accounts for differences in types of texts. He writes, "Every act of communication to or between human beings . . . presupposes a signification system that is its necessary condition. It is possible . . . to establish a semiotics of signification independently of a semiotics of communication; but it is impossible to establish a semiotics of communication without a semiotics of signification."[2] In other words, communication presupposes a system of signification, but a system of signification alone does not guarantee a meaningful act of communication.

---

2 Eco, *Theory of Semiotics*, 9.

A formal theory of codes comes under the heading of signification; the production of signs comes under the heading of communication. Codes arise from social convention. According to a famous analogy with chess in Wittgenstein, signification is like setting out chess pieces on a board and knowing the rules of chess; but no actual move has been made. The move itself is akin to a speech act that *makes use* of the signification in communication. Wittgenstein writes, "Naming is so far not a move in the language-game—any more than putting a piece in its place on the board is a move in chess. . . . *Nothing* has so far been done."[3] Conditions of signification are activated in what other writers might call hermeneutical life-worlds or speech-acts. Interaction occurs between the writer or sender and the code-system of the reader or receiver. Transient codes are usually sufficiently stable to make working dictionary definitions possible. Yet Eco argues that in poetry and in literary texts, generative strategies aim at "imprecise or undetermined response" on the basis of intertextual competence. Some texts invite "the *co-operation*" of their readers by compelling "interpretive choices."[4]

Some parables and some metaphors provide an excellent example of this process. Every text, says Eco, selects a "model reader," who may be a construct of the theory. The reader who is a "model" construct shares a selection of codes that have been *presupposed* by the author. In German hermeneutical writers this might be called their "preunderstanding." Eco observes, "Those texts [that] aim at arousing a precise response on the part of more or less empirical readers . . . are in fact open to any possible 'aberrant' decoding. A text not . . . 'open' to every possible interpretation will be called a *closed* one."[5] Thus, even a closed text can be misunderstood and misused by an "aberrant" decoding, if the interpreter has not fully understood the coding. Closed coding *aims* at precise communication but cannot *guarantee* intended communication. "Closed" texts, Eco argues, aim to pull the reader along a *predetermined*

3. Wittgenstein, *Philosophical Investigations*, sec. 49; cf. secs. 22 and 33.
4. Eco, *Role of the Reader*, 4.
5. Eco, *Role of the Reader*, 8.

path in order to arouse specific emotions and effects. These clearly include mass-advertising formats, comic strips, soap-opera romances, and Westerns. By contrast, James Joyce's *Finnegan's Wake* represents an "open" text, which embodies generative processes within its own structure. Some texts, Eco observes, are aimed at a general audience, for example, some political speeches and scientific instructions. In others an author may aim at a specific reader, for example, in a private letter.[6]

Eco distinguishes between various types of situations, for example, states of affairs, unverifiable hypotheses, and fiction. We might think of them as boxes or positions from which one reads. The point is that readers may need to "switch" from box to box, in accordance with what role the reader needs to play, and what choices the reader makes. These may be active or passive, filling out textual characterizations. The reader has to select from the right frame. In the case of a narrative the reader may have to wonder about the next step of a given story.[7] Eco is trying to avoid both undue subjectivism and undue objectivism. Not everyone, however, accepts his starting point of a distinction between open and closed texts. William Ray, for example, argues that we have reached an impasse caused by Eco seeking to have the best of both incompatible worlds.[8]

Yet on one side Eco recognizes legitimate constraints imposed on readers in closed or transmissive texts; while on the other hand he also recognizes the unpredictable pluralism stressed by Gadamer in open or literary texts. He makes a genuine advance by recognizing the very wide range of models that constitute texts, ranging from the simplest functional transmissive system used in engineering through to complex matrices of productive systems of literary meaning.

Eco uses a simple introductory model of the "transmissive" reading of a pointer on a dial on a control panel. This is mechanically

6. Eco, *Role of the Reader*, 9–11.

7. Eco, *Role of the Reader*, 27 and 33.

8. Ray, *Literary Meaning*, 134. Tremper Longman also has reservations, in *Literary Approaches to Biblical Interpretation*, 38.

linked to a floating buoy in order to indicate water level or fuel level. Even in this example, a dial rests on a social convention; one that is so widespread today that it is virtually trans-cultural (except in cultures that have no plumbing or traffic vehicles). An ancient culture might not recognize the basis on which the signifying system functions, but almost all modern cultures would presuppose the code that allows the pointer to communicate data. Differences between and within codes may entail "sub-codes." Eco points out the purely transmissive function of indicating a high water level as a fact. This differs from communicating some judgements about its significance, namely what level constitutes a flood warning or a danger level. Sub-codes may require a professional training. This training becomes a matter of "reader-competency," when we consider more productive or literary texts. John Barton rightly observes that reader-competency demands sufficient mastery of code to allow communicative or productive meaning in the case of biblical texts.

In productive texts the semantic function leads on to an advance that characterizes the infinity of chains of signs in the dictionary, the function of which is to catch "transient revaluations" of language uses.[9] This is one difference from handbook or transmissive texts. The distinction explored by Eco prevents his version of reader-response becoming as subjective and unconstrained as those, for example, of Stanley Fish, David Bleich, Norman Holland, and others. Norman Peterson writes, "Reader-response criticism warns actual readers to be wary of . . . seduction by an under coded text [i.e. one that allows too much ambiguity]."[10] Peterson cites an example in the text of Mark where Mark 13:14 has the well-known "wink," "let the reader understand." This allows readers to recognize themselves as "encoded in the text," which frames language about believers under persecution in this apocalyptic discourse.[11]

9. Eco, *Semantics and the Philosophy of Language*, 68–86

10. Peterson, "Reader in the Gospel," 41.

11. Peterson, "Reader in the Gospel," 45.

2. The Second Stage: Paul Ricoeur on Different Forms and Their Diverse Functions in Biblical Literature

In some ways it is arbitrary to intrude suddenly into Paul Ricoeur's thought in his mid-career in 1980, with his *Essays in Biblical Interpretation* (1980). We must also try not to anticipate too much our dialogue with Ricoeur in chapter 4. Ricoeur (1913–2005) was born at Valence in France of a committed Protestant family. He studied philosophy in 1934 at the Sorbonne, where he came under the influence of Gabriel Marcel, who especially valued the uniqueness of each human self. In 1939 he served in the French army but was taken prisoner by the Germans in 1940. As a prisoner of war, he chose to study three German philosophers: Karl Jaspers, Edmund Husserl, and Martin Heidegger. Together with Marcel, after the war, he researched into the human self, time, existence, and possibility. He received his doctorate from Strasbourg in 1950 and became Professor of Philosophy at the Sorbonne in 1956. His earliest books concerned the human will, guilt, finitude, and symbol. They are translated as *Fallible Man* (1965), *Freedom and Nature* (1966), and *The Symbolism of Evil* (1969). Later he would produce many works, including the magisterial *Time and Narrative* (3 vols, 1983) and the major study, *Oneself as Another* (1996).

Ricoeur's work on symbol and subsequently also on metaphor shows his interest in "open" texts, but also his concern to subcategorize open texts into symbol, metaphor, and other types of texts. He further insists that diverse biblical genres should not be treated as one kind of thing. In his essay "Toward a Hermeneutic of the Idea of Revelation," he comments, "It is from this amalgamation and this contamination that the massive and impenetrable concept of 'revealed truth' arises." Moreover, he also expresses it in the plural, "revealed truths," to emphasize "the discursive character of the dogmatic propositions that are taken to be identical to the founding faith."[12] He admits that this propositional form is "the original nucleus of the traditional idea of revelation," for it

---

12. Ricoeur, "Toward a Hermeneutic of the Idea of Revelation," 74.

represents the prophetic mode of discourse in which "the prophet presents himself as not speaking in his own name, but in the name of another."[13] Yet we must separate this prophetic mode of discourse from others, for example, from narrative; otherwise we risk imprisoning the idea of revelation in too narrow a concept.

The *narrative* mode of discourse, Ricoeur observes, "dominates the Pentateuch, as well as the Synoptic Gospels and the Book of Acts."[14] Theoreticians of narrative discourse have noted that, in the words of Ricoeur, "[i]n narration the author often disappears and it is as though the events recounted themselves."[15] It is as if the events tell themselves. Narrative leads to reflection on the events recounted. In the Old Testament this means, in the Pentateuch, Abraham and the exodus, and, later, the anointing of David. These characters and events "mark an epoch and engender history" and are "history-making events."[16] They are epoch-making because they relate to the founding of a community and its deliverance from a great danger.

Ricoeur alludes to Gerhard von Rad and "the theology of traditions" to illustrate the community-forming role of narrative. Von Rad refers to the Hebraic *Credo* in Deuteronomy 26:3b–10b, which begins, "My father was a wandering Aramamaean. He went down to Egypt to find refuge there, few in numbers, but there he became a nation, great, mighty, and strong. . . . He called on Yahweh, the God of our fathers. Yahweh heard our voice, and saw our misery, our toil, and our oppression, and Yahweh brought us out of Egypt" (Jerusalem Bible). The recitation first designates Yahweh (God) in the third person, but it rises to the second person as God acts. Similarly it begins with Israel in the third person, but changes to the first-person plural as they become increasingly involved. Ricoeur comments, "What is essential in the case of narrative discourse is the emphasis on the founding event or events as the imprint of marks or trace of God's act. Quotation

13. Ricoeur, "Toward a Hermeneutic of the Idea of Revelation," 75.
14. Ricoeur, "Toward a Hermeneutic of the Idea of Revelation," 77.
15. Ricoeur, "Toward a Hermeneutic of the Idea of Revelation," 77.
16. Ricoeur, "Toward a Hermeneutic of the Idea of Revelation," 78.

takes place through narration and the problematic of inspiration is in no way a primary generation. God's mark is in history before being in speech."[17]

Ricoeur stresses the specificity of narrative discourse to guard us from undue narrowness in a theology of the Word, and "word events." Here he explicitly approves of Wolfhart Pannenberg's stress on history as opposed to Fuchs and Ebeling on "word event."[18] Yet narration does also include prophecy as history moves forward in accordance with God's purposes towards the "Day of Yahweh," while allowing for a certain tension between narrative and prophecy. Revelation is implied in the narrative. Narrative implies teleology and providence. Ricoeur writes much more on narrative in *Time and Narrative,* as we shall see later.

Prophetic discourse and narrative both speak of "the will of God." The third mode of discourse arises as *"prescriptive discourse,"* which leads us into the realm of law and command.[19] Its characteristic mood is the imperative. It involves, Ricoeur writes, submission to a higher, external command. Yet it does not simply imply heteronomy (see glossary). He writes further, "The idea of dependence is essential to the idea of revelation."[20] But Ricoeur criticizes both autonomy and heteronomy. On one side, law is an expression of covenant in the Pentateuch. But on the other side, this also encompasses the ideas of grace, election, and promise. The Psalms witness to "the veneration of a joyous soul."[21] Ricoeur adds, "The Torah unfolds within a dynamism that we may characterize as historical."[22] These literary genres are distinct but also clearly overlap. Prescriptive discourse includes not only outward acts and behavior, but also matters of the heart. This led to the concept of the new covenant, especially in Jeremiah and Ezekiel, and throughout in the New Testament, especially in 2 Corinthians.

17. Ricoeur, "Toward a Hermeneutic of the Idea of Revelation," 79.

18. Ricoeur, "Toward a Hermeneutic of the Idea of Revelation," 80.

19. Ricoeur, "Toward a Hermeneutic of the Idea of Revelation," 81–82.

20. Ricoeur, "Toward a Hermeneutic of the Idea of Revelation," 82.

21. Ricoeur, "Toward a Hermeneutic of the Idea of Revelation," 83.

22. Ricoeur, "Toward a Hermeneutic of the Idea of Revelation," 83.

This deepening of the law beyond scattered precepts led on to the fourth mode of discourse, namely *wisdom discourse*. At first this involves practical counsel on how to live well. It concerns every person, and according to Ricoeur it includes those who live in solitude, suffering, death, misery, or where "the grandeur of human beings" confronts sorrow and pain.[23] He alludes to Jaspers's "limit situations." These may even include the supposed absence or silence of God, and both human affairs and the cosmos, or the sphere of the world. Further, all this "teaches us how to endure, how to suffer suffering. It places suffering into a meaningful context by producing the active quality of suffering."[24] Of this the book of Job is one example. Even here Job's questions about justice "are left without an answer."[25] God's design remains his secret.

Sometimes the lyric genre, which Ricoeur calls "*hymnic discourse,*" is neglected, in spite of the huge scope of the Psalms, where praise, supplication, and thanksgiving "constitute its three major genres. Clearly they are not marginal forms of religious discourse."[26] The wisdom discourse in Job becomes surpassed by the lyricism of praise. Ricoeur writes that in the Psalms "The invocation reaches its highest purity, its most disinterested expression, when supplication, unburdened of every demand, is converted into recognition. Thus under the three figures of praise, supplication, and thanksgiving, human speech becomes invocation. It is addressed to God in the second person."[27] The worshipper may use the first person "I" or "we."

These varied genres are crucial to hermeneutics. They are not some mere "rhetorical façade," which we could pull down.[28] Their differences are hermeneutically and theologically significant. Ricoeur concludes, "The notion of revelation may no longer be formulated in a uniform and monotonous fashion which we

23. Ricoeur, "Toward a Hermeneutic of the Idea of Revelation," 86.
24. Ricoeur, "Toward a Hermeneutic of the Idea of Revelation," 86.
25. Ricoeur, "Toward a Hermeneutic of the Idea of Revelation," 87.
26. Ricoeur, "Toward a Hermeneutic of the Idea of Revelation," 88.
27. Ricoeur, "Toward a Hermeneutic of the Idea of Revelation," 89.
28. Ricoeur, "Toward a Hermeneutic of the Idea of Revelation," 90.

presuppose when we speak of *the* biblical revelation."[29] Revelation and the biblical writings are a "polysemic and polyphonic concept." We must not generalize in a univocal fashion.

3. Third Stage: Varieties of Parables: Dodd, Jeremias, Linnemann, and Jülicher on Similes and Metaphors

The genre or category of parable invites special attention for at least three reasons. First, parables are not exclusive to the biblical writings, and occur in many different contexts, both secular and religious. Second, they illustrate very well how many sub-genres are grouped within this single term. Many of them function with diametrically opposite hermeneutical purposes. Third, a vast literature by hermeneutical and literary experts from many centuries has provided enormous collected wisdom on which we can draw.[30]

In 1935 one of the most famous definitions of parable was coined by Charles H. Dodd and was later repeated in part by Robert Funk. Dodd wrote, "At its simplest the parable is a metaphor or simile drawn from nature or common life, arresting the hearer by its vividness or strangeness, and leaving the mind in sufficient doubt about its precise application to tease the mind into active thought."[31] In Funk's words, "The parable is not closed so to speak until the listener is drawn into it as a participant."[32] On the other hand, some parables simply do not fit into this category of "open" texts. The meaning of some parables is meant to be self-evident. Thus, commenting on Jülicher's attempt to distinguish between metaphor, simile, parable, similitude, allegory, and so on, Joachim Jeremias described this as "a fruitless labour in the end since the Hebrew *māshāl* and the Aramaic *mathla* embraced all these

29. Ricoeur, "Toward a Hermeneutic of the Idea of Revelation," 92.

30. In addition to more than a thousand primary sources, cf. Kissinger, *Parables of Jesus.*

31. Dodd, *Parables of the Kingdom*, 16.

32. Funk, *Language, Hermeneutic and Word of God*, 133.

categories and many more without distinction."[33] He adds that the Hebrew and Aramaic words could include, for example: "parable, similitude, allegory, fable, proverb, apocalyptic revelation, riddle, symbol, pseudonym, fictitious person, example, argument, apology, refutation, and jest."[34] This statement is uncontroversial and correct. Amos Wilder also writes, "Jesus uses figures of speech in an immense number of ways. . . . Indeed we may say that the term 'parable' is misleading since it suggests a single pattern and often distorts our understanding of this or that special case."[35]

Perhaps we might begin with the contrast between the parable proper and the allegory. Eta Linnemann calls attention to some usual key differences. First, the parable functions to address and convince "outsiders," whereas allegory is addressed to "insiders." No code lies behind the allegory. They know how to apply or interpret it. She writes: "Allegories . . . serve to transmit encoded information which is only intelligible to the initiated."[36] Second, parables convey a *coherent* story from everyday life, usually taken from nature or from everyday life. Allegories offer a string of encoded applications that may not cohere together as an intelligible story.

Examples of both kinds of texts abound in the Old Testament and the New. Nathan tells David a coherent story about a selfish rich man who would not take from his abundant flock of sheep to feed a guest, but stole his neighbor's precious ewe lamb. He then pronounced, "You are the man" (2 Sam 12:1–15). Nathan would not have been wise to accuse an oriental king of adultery directly to his face. But the injustice of the story overwhelmed King David; the parable, so to speak, "wounds from behind," as an indirect discourse. Hence, this narrative operates as a parable proper.

By contrast, in Ezekiel 17:1–10 we read of a "mighty eagle," who represents King Nebuchadnezzar, which comes to "Lebanon," which represents Jerusalem. His seizure of the "topmost branch of

33. Jeremias, *Parables of Jesus*, 20.
34. Jeremias, *Parables of Jesus*, 20.
35. Wilder, *Early Christian Rhetoric*, 81.
36. Linnemann, *Parables of Jesus*, 7.

a cedar" is clearly not part of a coherent story but represents the fate of Jehoiachin. This is an *allegory, addressed to the initiated.* It does not contain a coherent narrative world but represents a string of representations. Even this contrast, however, is not entirely clear cut, for the parables of Jesus include at least some examples of allegories, as we shall see.

In English literature *The Pilgrim's Progress* by John Bunyan (1678) draws on a host of allegories. John Bunyan's interpreter speaks of a room, but this represents the Holy Spirit cleansing the human heart. By contrast, in the Parable of the Lost Coin (Luke 18:8-9) a real everyday woman sweeps a genuine everyday room to find a coin. The Parable of the Prodigal Son (Luke 15:11-32) remains a coherent story, until the "father" is read as "God," at which point the parable becomes an allegory. The Parable of the Laborers in the Vineyard and the employer (Matt 20:1-16) remains a parable. Each worker receives an agreed-upon day's wage. But when the employer generously grants the same wage to those who had worked for only one hour, the other workers are shocked and envious. Grace (symbolized by the free generosity of the employer) has eclipsed expectations of natural justice. There is little or no need to allegorize this parable.

A few parables are mixed. Sometimes one evangelist tells a story as a parable, and another tells it as an allegory. In Luke 14:16-24 the evangelist tells a coherent story of a great supper. The host sends out invitations that are refused. So the owner of the house instructs his servant "to bring in the poor, the crippled, the blind, and the lame" (v. 21). The purpose of the parable is to address outsiders, either Pharisaic critics or outcasts. However, in Matthew 22:1-10, Matthew begins with the coherent world of the parable: the same invitations are sent, and the same refusals received, but the host is now "a king" who gave a wedding banquet. Here the reaction to the refusals becomes disproportionate for a coherent story. "He sent his troops . . . and burnt their city" (v. 7). Now this has become an allegory depicting the fall of Jerusalem.

In the history of research on the parables Adolf Jülicher (1857-1938) long ago, in *Die Gleichnisreden Jesu* (1888), maintained that the original form used by Jesus was the simile, not the metaphor. Unlike metaphor or allegory, the simile needs no interpretation. He writes, "The similitude appeals to what has happened only once. . . . It only speaks of established facts."[37] The Parable of the Mustard Seed (Matt 13:31–32) belongs to this category. He insists that a parable has only one central point, unlike an allegory, which may contain a string of independent evaluations. Jülicher insisted that the simile functions as direct or literal speech while metaphor functions as indirect or non-literal speech. For direct speech he uses the German words *eigentliche Rede*, and for indirect speech or metaphor he used *uneigentliche Rede*.

Whether the play on words (indirect and inauthentic) was accidental we cannot now know, but the fact remains that he also claims that metaphor is "inauthentic speech" (*uneigentliche Rede*), while simile is "authentic speech" (*eigentliche Rede*) in the original teaching of Jesus. Metaphors, Jülicher thought, were a creation of the early church. Jülicher's views had enormous influence on New Testament scholarship for many years until, more recently, it was acknowledged that his claims were far too sweeping. We shall note that these run generally counter to the arguments of Fuchs, Funk, and others, on metaphor.

4. Fourth Stage: Jones, Via, Crossan, Fuchs, and Funk on Modern Participants and Readers

Research in hermeneutics has provided insights especially in the interpretation of "open" or reader-involvement parables for today. In his book *The Art and Truth of the Parables*, Geraint Vaughan Jones expounds the existential dimensions of the Parable of the Forgiving Father and the Prodigal Son (Luke 15:11–32).[38] He traces the younger son's "flight into estrangement and return through longing." He adds, "He finds life empty and meaningless without personal relationships, and he seems desperate. . . . Nobody wants

---

37. Jülicher, *Die Gleichnisreden Jesu*, 1:97.
38. Jones, *Art and Truth of the Parables*, 175.

him."[39] Even after his return the elder son treats him not as a person, but as a type. The new self, living in destitution, is "different from the competent, defiant, self at the moment of departure. . . . He is a stranger, unwanted and anonymous, experiencing the Artur Norcia of dereliction."[40] In other words, Jones anticipates later, modern, existential themes of depersonalization, estrangement, and the effect of personal decision upon the self. The prodigal's supposed friends were bound to him by the flimsiest of bonds—money. The father in the story restores his personhood, of which his gifts of the robe and the ring are indicators. Jones helpfully bridges any possible gap between the horizon of the text and the horizon of the modern world.

Dan Otto Via and many others also call attention to "plot" within the parables, as Ricoeur does more widely in narratives as such. The "tragic" parables, Via says, represent a story with a downward movement to disaster, while "comic" plots achieve the reverse, namely an upward dynamic. *Comic* parables include the Parable of the Dishonest Manager (Luke 16:1–9) and the Forgiving Father and Prodigal Son (Luke 15:11–32). *Tragic* parables include the Parables of the Talents (Matt 25:14–30) and of the Ten Maidens (Matt 25:1–13). The one-talent man perceives himself as a victim, exclaiming, "I knew that you were a harsh man." He refuses to take the risk of venture, or to reach a life-changing decision. The consequence of this action is that his rejection of taking responsibility leads to his loss of opportunity: he is not given to rule over cities like the others, who acted with courage and determination.[41] Similarly the foolish maidens "presumptuously believed that their well-being was guaranteed . . . that someone else will pay the bill."[42] This approach, like that of Jones, anticipates existential themes concerning human existence, together with a clear narrative plot. In his latest work Via shows increasing concern for structuralist approaches to the parables and other texts.

39. Jones, *Art and Truth of the Parables*, 185.
40. Jones, *Art and Truth of the Parables*, 175.
41. Via, *Parables*, 120.
42. Via, *Parables*, 126.

The Irish-American writer John Dominic Crossan expounds "parables of reversal" in his book *In Parables* (1973).[43] In the Parable of the Good Samaritan (Luke 10:25–37), he explains, the hearers confront the impossible in which "their world is turned upside down."[44] They had expected the Samaritan to be "bad," and the priest to be "good," but they have to rethink their values from the ground up. This is not a mere example story, because if it were one the priest and Levite (though certainly not the Samaritan) would normally be expected to play the role of the hero. If it had been intended as an example parable, Crossan writes, "For such a purpose it would have been far better to have made the wounded man a Samaritan and the helper a Jewish man outside clerical circles. But when good (clerics) and bad (Samaritan) become, respectively, bad and good, their old world is being challenged and we are faced with polar reversal."[45] The parable challenges the assumptions and more conventional values of the hearers.

Other parables of reversal include the Rich Man and Lazarus (Luke 16:19–31) and the Pharisee and the Tax Collector (Luke 18:10–14).[46] The piety of the Pharisee is expressed in his words about fasting twice on the Sabbath and his giving, which would not have been interpreted as arrogance by the hearers of the parable. For modern readers there is a problem. After centuries of Christian tradition, we are accustomed to thinking of Pharisees, at worst, as arrogant hypocrites. In this case the parable would function as a cosy moral tale. It would simply confirm a judgement upon hypocrisy.

In the first century, however, Judaism expected their role to be the very reverse: Pharisees were especially pure and set apart as sanctified; tax-collectors were notoriously greedy for whatever rake-off they could gain.[47] So in terms of a first-century audience the normal expectations are reversed by the parable. The

43. Crossan, *In Parables*, 53–78.
44. Crossan, *In Parables*, 65.
45. Crossan, *In Parables*, 64.
46. Crossan, *In Parables*, 66–69.
47. Cf. Thiselton, *Two Horizons*, 10–17.

supposedly "good" person is condemned, and "bad" person (the tax-collector) justified!

Walter Wink makes precisely this point in his book *The Bible in Human Transformation*.[48] As for Crossan, after a helpful beginning in *In Parables*, he turns increasingly to postmodernism in his later works, including *The Dark Interval* (1975), *Raid on the Articulate* (1976), *Cliffs of Fall* (1980), and contributions to the journal *Semeia*.

Ernst Fuchs and Robert Funk expound the "narrative world" of many parables, and Funk writes on the parable as metaphor. Funk writes, "Ernst Fuchs' effort to grasp the parables as language-events is the underground spring which nourishes my own approach to the parables."[49] He notes that Jülicher's emphasis on similes risks the danger of reducing parables to ciphers that transmit single abstract ideas in a historically concrete form. For Funk, all parables are open texts, the meaning of which must be completed by the hearer or reader.[50]

Meanwhile Fuchs insists that the parables of Jesus are active "masters," which address the hearer through "the language-event" (*Sprachereignis*), as Gadamer and Heidegger also argue. We saw that for Fuchs hermeneutics is not merely theoretical but practical. He compared hermeneutics to placing a mouse in front of a cat: it causes the cat to show itself for what it is.[51] Jesus, Fuchs maintains, created an empathy (*Einvertändnis*) with his hearers, by presenting "the world of the parable" to them. Like J. L. Austin's performative utterances, the word becomes a *speech act*: it promises, pledges, and offers (i.e., it *does* something, or performs an action).[52] He writes, "The text is therefore not just the slogans that transmit charismatic formulations, but rather, the master that directs us into the language-context of our existence."[53] His close colleague

48. Wink, *Bible in Human Transformation*, 42–43.

49. Funk, *Language, Hermeneutic, and Word of God*, 128.

50. Funk, *Language, Hermeneutic, and Word of God*, 133.

51. Fuchs, *Hermeneutik*, 109–10.

52. Fuchs, *Studies of the Historical Jesus*, 196.

53. Fuchs, *Studies of the Historical Jesus*, 211.

Gerhard Ebeling insists, "*The text . . . becomes a hermeneutic aid in the understanding of present experience*."[54] The text "speaks" to the present situation.

Fuchs and Ebeling reject the notion of language as a mere technical instrument. Fuchs declares, "Language makes Being into an event."[55] Language, he says, gathers Being, and "*brings into language the gathering of faith*."[56] This "gathering" effect is seen in the parables. Fuchs writes, "Jesus draws the hearer over to his side by means of the artistic medium, so that the hearer thinks together with Jesus. Is this not the way of true love? Love does not just blurt out. Instead, it provides in advance the sphere in which meeting takes place."[57]

The parable has created a "narrative world" in which the hearer may meet with Jesus, who has told the parable. The hearer participates in this world, rather than simply observing it. Readers yield themselves to this world, and the world acts on them. The parable is not a mere set of concepts to be manipulated by a spectator, not a mere object of scrutiny, but a "world" that takes hold of the hearer as someone who enters into it.[58] Conventional everyday presuppositions about life and reality may be challenged and shattered. On the Parable of the Labourers in the Vineyard (Matt 20:1–16) Fuchs writes, "We too share the inevitable reaction of the first [labourers]. The first see that the last receive a whole day's wage, and actually they hope for a higher rate for themselves."[59] But then comes the shock: "In fact they received the same. . . . It seems to them that the lord's action is unjust." Finally comes the verdict on this assumption: "Is your eye evil because I am kind?" Fuchs concludes, "Jesus pledges himself to those who, in place of a cry 'guilty,' nevertheless found their hope on an act of

---

54. Ebeling, *Word and Faith*, 33 (his italics).

55. Fuchs, *Studies of the Historical Jesus*, 207.

56. Fuchs, *Studies of the Historical Jesus*, 208–9.

57. Fuchs, *Studies of the Historical Jesus*, 129.

58. Fuchs, *Studies of the Historical Jesus*, 92.

59. Fuchs, *Studies of the Historical Jesus*, 33.

God's kindness."[60] The creative language-event takes place in the shared "narrative-world" of the parable. Robert Funk takes these comments as his point of departure for his work on the parable as metaphor.

Robert Funk presses as far as possible the "open" function of parables. He claims that on this basis "[i]t is not possible to specify once and for all what the parables mean."[61] Nevertheless, he does agree that there is a different function between parable as simile and parable as metaphor. He writes, "In simile it is illustrative; in metaphorical language it is creative of meaning. In simile as illustration the point to be clarified or illuminated has already been made and can be assumed; in metaphor the point is discovered."[62] He compares the distinction made here to C. S. Lewis's demarcation between a master's metaphor and a pupil's metaphor. He writes,

> The "magisterial" metaphor is one invented by the master to explain the point for which the pupil's thought is not yet adequate; it is therefore optional insofar as the teacher is able to entertain the same idea without the support of the image.
>
> On the other hand understanding itself emerges with the "pupillary" metaphor, with which it is consequently bound up; the "pupillary" metaphor is indispensable to the extent that understanding could not and cannot be reached in any other way. This distinction is also paralleled by Ian Ramsay's differentiation between a picture model and a disclosure model.[63]

For Funk the parable proper is always creative of understanding. Metaphor, he says, "raises the potential for new meaning. . . . Metaphor involves a 'soft,' as opposed to a 'sharp' focus."[64] Metaphor, he

60. Fuchs, *Studies of the Historical Jesus*, 33–37.

61. Funk, *Language, Hermeneutic, and Word of God*, 135.

62. Funk, *Language, Hermeneutic, and Word of God*, 137.

63. Funk, *Language, Hermeneutic, and Word of God*, 137; cf. Lewis, "Bluspels and Flanansferes," 36–50; and Ramsey, *Models and Mystery*, 9ff.

64. Funk, *Language, Hermeneutic, and Word of God*, 138.

continues, "shatters the conventions of predication in the interests of a new vision, one that grasps the 'thing' in relation to a new 'field', and thus in relation to a fresh experience of reality." He adds, "The metaphor is a means of modifying the tradition."[65]

In parables, Funk declares, "The word presents the reference in such a way that the listener is confronted by it; the auditor does not make a distinction between the vocables [stretches of language] and the reality of which the vocables give presence. Word and reality are encountered in their inner unity. Language becomes event."[66] Fuchs stands as a decisive influence here. The metaphor "embodies a 'world'."[67] In addition, Gadamer and the later Heidegger also stand in the background. Although we may query whether the meaning of the parable can never be expressed, it is surely correct when Funk says, "The 'meaning' of the parable cannot be fully articulated."[68] He repeats the point:

> The metaphor, like the parable, is incomplete until the hearer is drawn into it as participant; this is the reason why the parables are said to be argumentative, calling for a transference of judgement. Metaphor and parable sustain their existential tenor because they participate in immediacy, and immediacy pertaining to the future as well as to the present and past.[69]

He concludes, "The parables . . . have an imaginative and poetical quality. They are works of art and a serious work of art has significance beyond its original occasion."[70]

Funk adds, "The mystery of the paradox of the kingdom upsets the conventions, the standards of the common judgement."[71] Further, "The parables as pieces of everydayness could have an

65. Funk, *Language, Hermeneutic, and Word of God*, 139.
66. Funk, *Language, Hermeneutic, and Word of God*, 140.
67. Funk, *Language, Hermeneutic, and Word of God*, 140.
68. Funk, *Language, Hermeneutic, and Word of God*, 142.
69. Funk, *Language, Hermeneutic, and Word of God*, 143.
70. Funk, *Language, Hermeneutic, and Word of God*, 150.
71. Funk, *Language, Hermeneutic, and Word of God*, 155.

unexpected 'turn' in them which looks through the commonplace to a new view of reality."[72]

Funk proceeds to cite the Parable of the Great Supper (Matt 22:2–10 and Luke 14:16–24, with a comparison in the Apocryphal Gospel of Thomas, Logion 64) as illustrating his point. Matthew and Luke apply the parable in different ways. Jeremias argues that the Great Supper has been transformed into an allegory of the plan of salvation by Matthew, whereas Luke (and the later Gospel of Thomas) retain the original emphasis given by Jesus.[73] Luke describes the invitations to the Great Supper, and the various excuses for declining the invitation. Hence, the host became angry and then invited "the poor, the crippled, the blind, and the lame" (v. 21), and finally whoever his servants could find (v. 23).

Matthew lists not only various excuses but also says, "They made light of it" (22:5). Eventually the "king" was enraged (v. 7a); "He sent his troops, destroyed those murderers, and destroyed their city" (v. 7b). Clearly Matthew has in mind more than declining an invitation to dinner. Admittedly some might claim that Jeremias and perhaps Funk exaggerate the differences. Probably Luke expected his readers to see more than a mere dinner-invitation. Matthew's high drama is more explicit. So from this angle Funk may reasonably claim that Matthew and Luke legitimate a reader-response approach. The parable does not become "closed" until an application is made. At the same time, Funk appears harsher than necessary when he says, "Matthew has 'corrected' the parable in view of the situation in the church of his time."[74] Funk also pursues this theme in some of the eleven essays later published in his book *Parables and Presence* (1982). The parables of Jesus are certainly not all transmissive, closed texts, and Matthew and Luke do not consider them so. But when Jesus says, "He who has ears, let him hear," he does not mean: "make whatever you like of it."

---

72. Funk, *Language, Hermeneutic, and Word of God*, 161

73. Jeremias, *Parables of Jesus*, 176

74. Funk, *Language, Hermeneutic, and Word of God*, 170

5. Further Work on Metaphors: Ricoeur and Soskice

I have explored different types of metaphors in my book *The Power of Pictures in Christian Thought* (2018). Like Funk and others, I distinguished between ornamental or illustrative uses of metaphors and those that were more creative and also interactive. Following Ricoeur, I discussed the interaction between two different semantic domains. I referred to Lakoff and Johnson, *Metaphors We Live By* (1980), and their definition: *"The essence of metaphor is understanding and experiencing one kind of thing in terms of another."*[75]

Janet Martin Soskice in *Metaphor and Religious Language* (1985) points out that definitions of metaphor had been offered since the pre-Socratic philosophers, and especially since Aristotle. She rightly dismisses the view that metaphors are merely decorative. Ornamental metaphors, I have argued, do exist but they do not convey new truth, only make improvements stylistically, or make already familiar truths more vivid. Soskice also rejects accounts that depend on the "substitution theory." The substitution theory of metaphor claims that a metaphor is substituted for what could otherwise be expressed in plain speech. Such theories, Soskice argues, reduce metaphor to "no more than translating from a prior and literal understanding into an evocative formulation."[76]

So what is metaphor? Soskice adopts the view of Stephen Ullmann: "There are always two terms present: the thing we are talking about and that to which we are comparing it."[77] In metaphor we see one thing (perhaps even an unknown x) in terms of another, and this is genuinely enlightening.[78] War is a game of chess; a

75. Lakoff and Johnson, *Metaphors We Live By*, 5 (their italics).

76. Soskice, *Metaphor and Religious Language*, 24–53. Soskice contrasts a "theory-constitutive metaphor" (147).

77. Soskice, *Metaphor and Religious Language*, 20.

78. Though metaphor can mislead as well as enlighten. Heraclitus is said to have coined the metaphor "the river of time," which Wittgenstein demonstrated as having misleading consequences. Time as a flowing river suggests questions that we cannot answer, such as "Where did the past go to?" (*Blue Book*, 26–27).

camel is "the ship of the desert"; light travels in waves. The most important types of metaphor, she argues, are those that Max Black described as "interactive metaphors." These make possible incremental understanding and are both creative and often cognitive.

Paul Ricoeur published an influential book on metaphor, *The Rule of Metaphor* (1975, Eng., 1978), as well as numerous essays on the subject, including "Metaphor and Symbol" in his *Interpretation Theory* (Eng. 1976). He argues that both symbol and metaphor produce a "surplus of meaning"; both produce "a double-meaning"; and both yield an "extension of the meaning" of a word."[79]

Anticipating Soskice, Ricoeur excludes the notion of a theory of metaphor based on substitution, stressing the transformative and creative notion of metaphor.[80] When the semantic networks of two previously unlinked words engage one another in metaphor, meaning is born. And this can prove generative even for the scientific understanding of our world. E.g., light travels in waves; light travels in line. Here metaphor brings together two distinct realms, one linguistic and the other non-linguistic.[81] He further argues that symbols cannot be exhausted by merely conceptual language. Like Paul Tillich, he reasons that the extended meaning operates at a deeper pre-conceptual level. Like Wheelwright, he stresses the tensive character of creative metaphors. Wheelwright had written, "The essence of metaphor consists in the nature of the tension which is maintained among the heterogeneous elements brought together in one commanding image or expression."[82] Soskice offers the example of a "writhing script" in handwriting. But most metaphors exhibit this tension, e.g., "Achilles was a lion"; "Odysseus was a fox." For Ricoeur too

---

Metaphors can also die. E.g., illustrative metaphors such as "the neck of the bottle" or "the mouth of the river," which have become thinned down by frequent use.

79. Ricoeur, *Interpretation Theory*, 45 and 49.

80. Ricoeur, *Interpretation Theory*, 50.

81. Ricoeur, *Interpretation Theory*, 53–54.

82. Wheelwright, *Burning Fountain*, 101.

"[m]etaphor implies a tensive use of language in order to uphold the tensive concept of reality."[83]

Wheelwright and Ricoeur also draw upon I. A. Richards (1893–1973) and his distinction between "vehicle" and "tenor." The vehicle is the object whose attributes the metaphor borrows; the tenor is the attributes that are ascribed to it. In the previous example, lions in the jungle would be the vehicle; calling Achilles a lion would be the tenor. Some call this "intensive" meaning; others call it "extended" meaning.

Owen Barfield (1898–1997), philosopher of law and poet, makes the same point about the creative extension of meaning through legal fiction in his essay "Poetic Diction and Legal Fiction" (1945), to which Robert Funk also refers. Legal fiction comes into being when we need to extend the language to say what it strictly cannot say. Ordinary words are given an extended meaning with a fictional twist. Legal fictions may provide a deep feeling of liberation.

In his book *The Rule of Metaphor* Ricoeur states, "Metaphor presents itself as a strategy of discourse that, while preserving and developing the creative power of language, preserves and overlaps the *heuristic* power wielded by *fiction*."[84] He adds "split reference" to Roman Jakobson's notion of "split sense," speaking of "the intersection of spheres of discourse."[85] Split sense would be a split or division in meaning; split reference would be a split between the objects to which each refers. Ricoeur also speaks of metaphor as offering "a productive use of ambiguity."[86] It operates through "an interplay of similarity and dissimilarity."[87] This creative act of bringing together two distinct linguistic spheres in metaphor is brought to completion as the interpreter grasps, or is grasped by, the metaphor and new understanding is generated. As Ricoeur

---

83. Wheelwright, *Burning Fountain*, 68.

84. Ricoeur, *Rule of Metaphor*, 6 (his italics).

85. Ricoeur, *Rule of Metaphor*, 295–303.

86. Ricoeur, "Metaphor and Symbol," 47 and 49.

87. Ricoeur, "Metaphor and Symbol," 56.

concludes, *"Thus a metaphor does not exist in itself, but in and through an interpretation."*[88]

All of this combined work on metaphor vindicates the approach of Fuchs and Funk on the creative power of metaphor in parables, although it does not pretend to defend the universal application of this approach. We have seen that Adolph Jülicher was wrong to argue that all original parables were similes; but it would be equally wrong to insist that every single parable must have been a metaphor. Both categories of parable are genuinely operative, and a spectrum of meaning also operates between them. Where Fuchs and Funk are correct is in emphasizing the creative and productive power of metaphor, and the participatory nature of the response of the reader in these circumstances. Their point is valid but not without limit.

6. Further Types and Functions in *New Horizons in Hermeneutics*

In my book *The Two Horizons* (1980) I drew upon several philosophers and hermeneutical thinkers (especially Gadamer and Wittgenstein) to show how in hermeneutics the horizon of the text and its author could productively engage with the horizons of modern readers. But I became increasingly dissatisfied with generalizations about especially biblical texts and even about modern readers. I was especially uncomfortable with the abstract phrase "modern man." Twelve years later I was determined to consider what Wittgenstein called "the particular case" in terms of both texts and readers. So an entirely new book, entitled *New Horizons in Hermeneutics* appeared in 1992.

Horizons become new, in one sense, because readers' horizons expand when they engage with a text, especially the biblical text. Second, in hermeneutics the increasingly interdisciplinary nature of the subject forces an ever-widening horizon that embraces biblical studies, philosophy, linguistics, semiotics, literary

---

88. Ricoeur, "Metaphor and Symbol," 50 (Ricoeur's italics).

theory, speech-act theory, social sciences, liberation hermeneutics, and a variety of other disciplines. We comment on this in chapter 4, with reference to Ricoeur. Third, theories of reading make an impact on the transformative experiences of readers. Increasingly, interpreters focus on the effects of reading texts in certain ways. What *effects* do given texts produce on human thought and life? We noted above Schleiermacher's concern for this.

I could enumerate more ways in which horizons are "new," but these were specified in my introduction to *New Horizons in Hermeneutics* and further in a second edition twenty years later (2012). The main point, however, is the particularity of each horizon. As Ricoeur agrees, too often the biblical writings are treated as if they are a monochrome landscape. This comes to its clearest focus in chapters 15 and 16 on "The Hermeneutics of Pastoral Theology." Chapter 15 carries the subtitle "Ten Ways of Reading Texts in Relation to Varied Reading-Situations" and chapter 16 bears the subtitle, "Further Reading-Situations."

The first model or reading-situation related to what I called "enquiring reading." This looked back to an earlier chapter: "The Hermeneutics of Enquiry: From the Reformation to Modern Theory." I conceded that "reconstructionist" models[89] did not apply to *all* kinds of texts but were relevant to communicative texts and to questions asked by the Reformers. I tried to rescue the word "intention" in connection with authors. The concept of the author's intention has sometimes been regarded as discredited in relatively recent times. Some, especially literary critics, claimed that intention is merely an inner state of mind, which cannot be recaptured objectively, but only by intuition or guesswork. More than a few literary theorists thus consider talk of an author's intention as "the intentional fallacy." But we can in a large part restore its credibility by speaking of "intentional directedness." Ricoeur and others point out that all discourse (notably address) is *directed*

---

89. In hermeneutics "reconstructionist models" denote those methods that seek to go behind the text to recapture the intention and aim of the author, often by historical reconstruction. Betti is among those who use this term with approval.

toward a end. Hence, Ricoeur emphasizes the place of the *will* in communication. Language is not simply expressive, as if humans were animals!

The linguistic philosopher Wittgenstein observes, "Only in the stream of thought and life do words have meaning."[90] "Intention" does itself no favors when it functions simply as an abstract noun. "Intention" is better understood as an *adverb*: *to write with an intention is to write in a way that is directed towards goal.* We shall return in chapter 4 to Ricoeur's view on the place of the directed *will* of an author.

The aims of Schleiermacher and Dilthey were not to seek historical reconstruction in a purely generic sense, but to enter and appreciate the life-world of the author. The philosopher of language and philosopher of mind, John Searle, implicitly recognizes the value of what he calls the "background" or the "pre-intentional" settings of meaning. He calls this "A set of preconditions of Intentionality. . . . The biological and cultural resources that I must bring to bear to this task" (i.e. of interpretation or reading).[91] He rejects the criticism of some literary theorists that "intention" is merely an abstract and artificial construction that in the context of interpretation serves no purpose.

The Reformers were right: the evangelists and apostles had definite aims in their writings, and these expressed an act of will and a goal. Hence, for many transmissive texts in the New Testament a "hermeneutics of enquiry" is appropriate. This does not in any way exclude the importance of literary texts. In the Gospels, for example, many parables are to be understood as literary texts (e.g., the parables of Jesus as narratives), not in terms of transmission alone.

Many biblical texts remain *transmissive and communicative,* expressing the thought of an author towards a given directedness. Would Paul, Luke, and John have said of their work, "Go and make whatever you like of this"? The New Testament proclaims a *kerygma* or a message. It states at its heart that Jesus died and was raised

90. Wittgenstein, *Philosophical Investigations,* sec. 173.

91. Searle, *Intentionality,* 143.

and is Lord. These are transmissive texts. But this is not to deny that they are *also self-involving*. The choice between transmissive and literary or self-involving texts is not an exclusive alternative. For instance, the confession "Jesus is Lord" (1 Cor 12:3) involves the speaker, as well as stating a fact. This constitutes a first model.

A second model concerns existential texts and existentialist interpretation. To confess Christ as Lord, as Rudolf Bultmann rightly observed, is to let the care of oneself go, to place oneself entirely in the sovereign hands of the one who is Lord: "If we live, we live to the Lord; and if we die, we die to the Lord; whether we live, therefore, or whether we die, we are the Lord's" (Rom 14:7). Bultmann writes, "The believer . . . no longer belongs to himself (1 Cor 6:19). He no longer bears the care of himself, for his own life, but let's this care go, yielding himself entirely to the grace of God: he recognises himself to be the property of God (or of the Lord) and lives for him."[92] In this context, he also cites 1 Corinthians 3:21–23, "All things are yours . . . ."

Yet Bultmann is wrong to imply that the factual can be translated into the existential *exhaustively and without remainder*. The existential emphasis does indeed relate to individuals, as Bultmann, Kierkegaard, and Jaspers stress. Biblical texts become individuating vehicles, as when God addressed Adam in Eden: "Where are you?" (Gen 3:9). Bultmann says that Adam hid among the trees of the garden, but "Man stands before God alone . . . in stark loneliness."[93] This runs parallel with Kierkegaard's saying, "The most ruinous evasion of all is to be hidden in the crowd in an attempt to get away from hearing God's voice as an individual."[94] One well-known example is Kierkegaard's wrestling with texts about Abraham (Gen 22:1–19) in *Fear and Trembling* (1843), and in particular the slaying of the son of promise, Isaac. Kierkegaard admitted that in theory it remains perfectly possible to pour out speech *about* Abraham and *about* Abraham's faith; but to admire this faith and to praise it is not necessarily to understand it.

92. Bultmann, *Theology of the New Testament*, 331.
93. Bultmann, *This World and Beyond*, 21.
94. Kierkegaard, *Purity of Heart Is to Will One Thing*, 163.

In *Point of View of My Work as an Author* Kierkegaard saw his own task as that of showing what it is *to live* the gospel rather than to think about it. A merely conventional and conceptual attempt to describe Abraham's plight would not hit the mark. The reader must become *involved* in the sharp edge of choice-in-the-face-of-paradox. Kierkegaard writes with tongue-in-cheek, "If the interpreter had known Hebrew, then perhaps it might have been easy for him to understand the story of Abraham."[95] Even Isaac could not fully understand, but Abraham "left his worldly understanding behind and took with him only faith."[96] Abraham "believed the ridiculous. . . . He knew that no sacrifice was too hard when God demanded it—and he drew the knife."[97] As in many existentialist writers, understanding runs its head against the limits of a conventional community world. Some biblical texts, but certainly not all, operate in this existential and self-involving way. This provides a second model of how some biblical texts operate. They do not leave the hearer or reader unchanged; they are transformative. We saw examples above from the parables in Dan Otto Via, Geraint Vaughan Jones, Ernst Fuchs, and to some extent in Robert Funk.

A third model is that of the narrative world, as evidenced in Gadamer, Crossan, and many narrative theorists. Today readers have become habituated to enter narrative worlds almost every day, through television or through reading fiction. They often suspend their own belief-systems or even their customary moral defences for the sake of being carried along by the flow of the story. Resistances or prejudices may become weaker. Millions choose to become caught up in the temporal flow of plots and subplots on television or in popular literature. In the classic parable-form, exemplified in Nathan's parable about the rich man who took his poor neighbors lamb (2 Sam 12:1–6), narratives can catch readers off-guard. Because the narrative entices them into its world and enthrals them, they become unconsciously exposed to viewpoints, judgements, and reversals of assumptions that in other modes of

95. Kierkegaard, *Fear and Trembling*, 44.
96. Kierkegaard, *Fear and Trembling*, 45; cf. 50.
97. Kierkegaard, *Fear and Trembling*, 54, 55.

discourse would have called explicitly on conscious willingness to be open to the text. Narrative can reverse expectations that initially would be hostile to its viewpoint.

Crossan's "parables of reversal" well-illustrate this approach. Narrative worlds also stimulate imagination and exploration of *possible* worlds, as Ricoeur has argued. In productive narrative worlds they will overlap with self-involving speech-acts. In these, speech acts or illocutions (see glossary) may also become operative. We noted that Ernst Fuchs draws on the notion of narrative-world to trace the hermeneutical function of the Parable of the Laborers and the Generous Employer (Matt 20:1–16).[98] The story-world engages with different people at a deeper-than-intellectual level. Fuchs also stresses that this approach may avoid negative confrontation and may illustrate the way of love in preparing a place of meeting for different, or initially hostile, viewpoints. However, it is important to understand that not all narrative-worlds subvert worlds (as some parables of Jesus do); some parables and the exodus narrative, say, *found* and *create* a world.

George Stroup declares, "Christian narrative assumes a literary form akin to that of confession or religious autobiography."[99] He writes, "Mark clearly demonstrates that one cannot know who Jesus is apart from the narrative of his personal history."[100] Story, or narrative, also provides a way of expanding and characterizing personhood in a unique way. To identify highly personal characteristics, we often tell stories about people as the people they are. To categorize or try to define someone in the abstract in terms of qualities does not perform the same task. As Ricoeur, above all, shows in his *Time and Narrative*, plot is crucial to narrative and narrative is crucial to identity.

A fourth model is that of biblical symbol. Northrop Frye observes in *The Great Code* (1982) how frequently the biblical writers speak symbolically of the city, the mountain, the river, garden,

98. Fuchs, *Studies of the Historical Jesus,* 32–38 and 154–56.

99. Stroup, *Promise of Narrative Theology,* 91.

100. Stroup, *Promise of Narrative Theology,* 161.

tree, oil, fountain, bread, wine, bride, sheep, and so on.[101] Carl Jung and Paul Tillich speak of symbols as archetypes, and Paul Ricoeur speaks of symbols as double-meaning expressions.[102] To speak of evil as a "burden" or as "bondage" is to interpret these terms within a trans-empirical (i.e. non-physical) framework, so that they operate at a higher or second level of meaning, often with added emotion. Evil can be symbolized as a "blot" or "stain," and sin as "deviation from a path."

Multi-signification, however, can also allow room for self-deception, and therefore symbols invite *critical* interpretation. Wrongly used, symbols may simply project the human will to create the values that we wish, which might serve self-interest. On the other hand, as Ricoeur stresses, symbols may creatively give rise to thought, and then to understanding. The critical dimension serves truth and explanation; the creative dimension serves production of meaning, imagination, and hermeneutics.

In Freud's analysis, dream-symbols can disguise the repressed wishes or contents of the unconscious; in Jung's view, they compensate for one-sided or absent features in consciousness, and perform a constructive role in the movement towards maturity and integration.[103] Tillich contrasts the fragmenting character of conceptual subject-object language with the integrating power of symbol, with its emphasis on wholeness.[104] He writes, "Religious symbols . . . are a representation of that which is unconditionally beyond the conceptual sphere." They transcend the realm "that is split into subjectivity and objectivity." Symbol "grasps our unconscious as well as our conscious being. It grasps the creative ground of our being."[105]

---

101. Frye, *Great Code*, xiii.

102. Ricoeur, *Interpretation Theory*, 45 and 55–57; and Ricoeur, *Conflict of Interpretations*, 287–334.

103. Rollins, *Jung and the Bible*, 24–26 and 37–40.

104. Tillich, *Dynamics of Faith*, 43–47; and Tillich, *Systematic Theology*, throughout

105. Tillich, *Shaking of the Foundations*, 86; and Tillich, "Religious Symbol," 303.

Jung argued that archetypal images include masculine figures—the father, giant, or ogre, together with the hero or noble knight—and feminine figures, including the mother, princess, the wicked queen, and the wise old woman. But he also stressed their value in the development of individuation: the process of "becoming one's own self." He argued that the healing power of symbols unleashes deeper forces, and that they are more than vehicles for the conscious thought-processes of argument. They evoke the depths of God, . . . not taught by human wisdom (1 Cor 2:10, 13). He also cites examples of the power of symbols in the book of Revelation: "The angel showed me the river of the water of life, bright as crystal, flowing from the throne of God and of the Lamb. . . . On either side of the river is the tree of life with its twelve kinds of fruit. . . . And the leaves of the tree are for the healing of the nations" (Rev 22:1, 2).[106]

The interpretation of symbols clearly constitutes an example where hermeneutical method cannot possibly follow a transmissive or literal model of texts. The model is entirely different from that of a narrative world and from existential interpretation as well as from transmissive communication. The four models so far outlined operate in entirely different ways, even if their functions and forms sometimes overlap. In *New Horizons in Hermeneutics*, I further discussed the fifth model of semiotic productivity, the sixth model of reader-response approaches, the seventh model of socio-critical theory, an eighth model of deconstruction, a ninth model of speech-act theory, and tenth model of "believing reading" with reference to Alfred Schutz's criteria of relevance in sociology.

It is unnecessary, however, to pursue in detail more than the first four models, which illustrate abundantly the impossibility of using the same hermeneutical model to interpret the wide variety of texts, whether biblical or secular.

There is more than needs to be said about narrative worlds. One thinks, for instance, of the work of Seymour Chatman and Gérard Genette on narrative time.[107] Chatman and Genette show

106. Jung, *Man and his Symbols*.

107. Chatman, *Story and Discourse*; and Genette, *Narrative Discourse*.

how differences in narrative time can enhance the "point" of a narrative. For example, the high speed of the early chapters in Mark and the very slow tempo of the Passion Narrative combine to show that the whole narrative of the gospel serves to show that the cross constitutes its key "point." Popular detective fiction depends a lot the use of flashbacks, as does Dickens' *Great Expectations*. But I have said enough for now to communicate my central point that narrative texts can create and subvert the worlds of their readers.

This chapter has been a cumulative argument, beginning with Lotman and Eco on open and closed texts, passing to Ricoeur's five distinctions on declarative, narrative, command, legal, and lyric or hymnic texts, then considering varieties of forms and functions of parables, and focusing on instances of parables of reversal and existential interpretation. We conclude that hermeneutical methods must be as various and contingent as the distinctive differences between human persons and their situations, as well as major differences between texts, whether biblical or not. One of the few writers to grasp this in detail has been Paul Ricoeur, and we shall conclude by examining his approach further.

Chapter 4

The Culmination of the Appeal
The Contribution of Ricoeur

I HOPE THAT THE arguments above for the need for hermeneutics will be convincing. Yet while many hold this conviction, there are some who do not. From 1992 until 2011 I taught hermeneutics as a core course in the University of Nottingham, with an extended part-time contract after I retired from the Chair of the Department. Earlier, I had also taught hermeneutics in the University of Sheffield from 1971 for some seventeen years. But although my Nottingham department and its students wanted me to continue, the university administration felt that hermeneutics did not justify a budgetary shortfall, and since 2011 hermeneutics has no longer appeared on the Nottingham course-options.

It is my hope that tracing points of affinity between my work and Paul Ricoeur will constitute a decisive culmination to my arguments for the importance and relevance of hermeneutics for every university course in theology and also perhaps for courses in philosophy and linguistics, if not in the humanities as a whole. As we saw from Emilio Betti, the qualities of patience, tolerance, humility, understanding, and an appropriate attitude to particular texts (especially where pluralism is a concern) ought to make hermeneutics a relevant discipline in all university humanities courses. Of the many points of affinity with Ricoeur, perhaps one of the most characteristic is his insistence that hermeneutics should always be a *multi-disciplinary* subject, so we shall begin with this.

1. Interdisciplinary Hermeneutics

Ricoeur does not merely engage with philosophy, but also with linguistics, concepts of selfhood, symbolism, theories of metaphor, understandings of narrative (including narrative voices and the notion of narrative identity), intersubjectivity, theology and biblical studies, and social science. His volume of essays *The Conflict of Interpretations* (1974) brings together structuralism, psychoanalysis, phenomenology, symbolism, and religion, as all being integral to hermeneutics. Don Ihde, the editor of this volume, writes, "The twenty-two essays which appear here span the period 1960–69. . . . This collection of essays is striking in its diversity: structuralism and linguistic analysis, hermeneutics and phenomenology, psychoanalysis, and the question of the subject, religion and faith, all are discussed."[1] Perhaps this is one of the reasons why hermeneutics does not feature in more British universities. Even in America I recall being invited to lecture in a seminary in California, where my interdisciplinary course not only frightened off my usual number of students, but the administration complained that the budget should belong exclusively to a regular single discipline, which they thought administratively necessary.

Ricoeur himself is explicit about multi-disciplinary studies in the subtitle of his book *The Rule of Metaphor: Multi-disciplinary Studies of the Creation of Meaning in Language* (1978). The subject also appears in his appendix, "From Existentialism to Philosophy of Language," where he traces his early focus on existential experiences of finitude and guilt through Husserl and phenomenology, and then Freud's psychoanalysis, to philosophy of language and semantics, including Anglo-American linguistic philosophy.[2]

---

1. Ricoeur, *Conflict of Interpretations*, ix; cf. Ihde, *Hermeneutic Phenomenology*.

2. Ricoeur, *Rule of Metaphor*, 315–22.

There are various inspirations for Ricoeur's concern with multi-disciplinary approaches. First, in the 1930s he studied under Gabriel Marcel (1889–1973) in Paris and was also influenced by Maurice Merleau-Ponty and others; then in the years of the Second World War, he studied the works of Jaspers and Heidegger. Merleau-Ponty, Jaspers, and Heidegger are all in some sense phenomenologists and existentialists. But they also have in common that they worked in more than one discipline.[3] This concern about multi-disciplinarity is further underlined when we recall how much of Ricoeur's initial motivation for hermeneutics arose from his notion of double-meaning, which was originally mainly drawn from Freud. He writes, "Psychoanalysis was also directly linked to linguistic perplexity [i.e. ambiguity]. . . . Are not dreams and symptoms some kind of indirect language?"[4] He adds, "The claim of psychoanalysis to explain symbols and myths as fruits of unconscious representations, as distorted expressions of the relation between nearby general impulses and the repressive structures of the super-ego compelled me to enlarge my first concept of hermeneutics beyond a mere semantic analysis of double-meaning expressions."[5]

In his book *Freud and Philosophy* (1970) Ricoeur makes one of his most important statements. He writes, "Hermeneutics seems to me to be animated by this double motivation: willingness to suspect, willingness to listen; vow of rigor, vow of obedience. In our time we have not finished doing away with *idols* and we have barely begun to listen to *symbols*."[6] Later in this work he will state another of his key sayings: "Symbols give rise to thought."[7] But, he adds, they also yield the birth of idols. As soon as he began to

---

3. Merleau-Ponty worked on the dignity and uniqueness of human beings as persons; Jaspers worked in psychiatry, psychotherapy, and limit-situations; and Heidegger included in his philosophy the impact of personal decision, being-in-the world, solicitude, and hermeneutics.

4. Ricoeur, *Rule of Metaphor*, 317.

5. Ricoeur, *Rule of Metaphor*, 318.

6. Ricoeur, *Freud and Philosophy*, 27 (his italics).

7. Ricoeur, *Freud and Philosophy*, 543.

reflect on levels or layers of meaning, Ricoeur immediately realized that psychoanalysis was entirely relevant to this. In psychoanalysis a patient is assisted in overcoming symptomatic behavior both through an explanatory process, which uses *causal* explanation, and through a deepened self-awareness and *understanding*. We immediately encounter the double focus of explanation (German, *Erklärung*) and understanding (*Verstehen*). We recall that Karl-Otto Apel devoted a whole book to this polarity of *Erklärung* and *Verstehen*.[8]

On Freud, Ricoeur writes, "Dreams constitute models of disguised, substituted, and fictive expressions of human wishing or desire."[9] What has to be "interpreted" is not the dream as dream, but the text of the dream as it is recounted. Psychoanalysis aims to recover the primitive speech of desire. Thus, dream provides a classic model of double meaning, characterized by a showing-hiding duality. Ricoeur regards this same showing-hiding duality to also characterize the revelation of God, who is both hidden and revealed. He says, "To interpret is to understand the double meaning."[10]

According to Freud, when the latent content of the dream-as-dream ("the dream thoughts") are transposed into the manifest content of the dream-as-remembered ("the dream content"), what is actually recounted may represent a "condensation" of the dream in a form that is "brief, meagre, and laconic." It may also reflect a "displacement," in which sequences and images become transformed and "scrambled" by the repression of the sensor, which protectively disguises the meaning of the symbols or images from the conscious mind. Psychoanalytical interpretation seeks to discover the deeper "text" below the dream-account, represented by the dream-thoughts.

These Freudian categories were developed by Roman Jakobson in linguistics in terms of metaphor and metonymy, condensation and displacement. These, Ricoeur agrees, "add tests on

8. Apel, *Understanding and Explanation*.

9. Ricoeur, *Freud and Philosophy*, 5.

10. Ricoeur, *Freud and Philosophy*, 8.

the plane of meaning to an 'overdetermination' which calls for interpretation."[11]

Ricoeur valued Freud's psychoanalysis, with its reductive element, in terms of an *explanatory* analysis of hermeneutics. He comments:

> Freud was only one of the exponents of the reductive hermeneutics. . . . Marx and Nietzsche and before them Feuerbach, had to be understood as the fathers of this reductive method. The claim of psychoanalysis to explain symbols and myths as fruits of unconscious representations, as distorted expressions of the relation between nearby general impulses and repressive structures of the super-ego compelled me to enlarge my first concept of hermeneutics beyond a mere semantic analysis of double meaning expressions.[12]

He adds:

> Hermeneutics appeared henceforth as a battlefield traversed by two opposing trends, the first tending toward a reductive explanation, the second tending toward a recollection or a retrieval of the original meaning of the symbol. My problem was to link these two approaches and to understand their relation as dynamic and as a moving from a first naïveté through critique to what I called at the time a second naïveté.[13]

Because of the intellectual situation in France, Ricoeur also turned his attention to semantics and to all the semiological disciplines. Nevertheless he recognized that hermeneutics calls into question "the idea that language is a closed system of signs, within which each element merely refers to the other elements of the system."[14] So he moved beyond semantics to engage with the post-Bultmannian hermeneutics of Fuchs and Ebeling. Finally, the concept of "God-talk" led him to examine British and American

11. Ricoeur, *Freud and Philosophy*, 93.
12. Ricoeur, *Rule of Metaphor*, 318.
13. Ricoeur, *Rule of Metaphor*, 318.
14. Ricoeur, *Rule of Metaphor*, 319.

linguistic philosophy, together with work on the parables by Jeremias, Via, and Perrin. Further, he wrote, "Ordinary language now appears to me, following the work of Wittgenstein and Austin, to be a kind of conservatory for expressions which have preserved the highest descriptive power as regards human experience, particularly in the realm of action and feelings."[15] In effect, this means that Ricoeur began to concern himself with what may be called conceptual analysis.

It is not only in *The Rule of Metaphor* that Ricoeur emphasizes multi-disciplinarity. In his volume *Hermeneutics and the Human Sciences* (1981) he considers the history of hermeneutics, explanation, and understanding together with metaphor, and studies in the philosophy of social science, including Freud and types of narrative. In his "Intellectual Autobiography" he stresses how in his book *Time and Narrative* (1984–88) he drew in the first volume on Augustine's *Confessions*, Aristotle's *Poetics*, and other sources, to explore the relation between concordance and discordance.[16] Among his later works, in his equally magisterial book, *Oneself as Another* (1992), Ricoeur discusses selfhood, personhood, narrative identity, and accountability, with reference to Descartes and Hume, to Recanati, Austin, and Searle; to Anscombe, Davidson, and Strawson; to Aristotle and Kant, to Locke, Hume, and Dilthey, and to many others. His main essays almost constitute a lecture on the history of philosophy. Almost every book of Ricoeur witnesses to the need for a multidisciplinary approach as groundwork for hermeneutics.

I entirely share these concerns. My first major book on hermeneutics, *The Two Horizons* (1980), approached the subject of hermeneutics in dialogue with four philosophers of different traditions: the earlier and later Heidegger, Bultmann the New Testament scholar, Hans Georg Gadamer on hermeneutics, and Ludwig Wittgenstein, a major exponent of conceptual analysis. One of my longest and more recent books, *Thiselton on Hermeneutics:*

15. Ricoeur, *Rule of Metaphor*, 319–20.

16. Ricoeur, "Intellectual Autobiography," 42; and Ricoeur, *Time and Narrative*, 1:5–90.

The Collected Works and New Essays of Anthony Thiselton (2006, 827 pages) was divided into seven parts: Part One on situating the subject; Part Two on hermeneutics and speech-act theory; Part Three on hermeneutics, semantics, and conceptual grammar; Part Four on lexicography, exegesis, and reception history; Part Five on parables, narrative-worlds, and reader-response theories; Part Six on philosophy, language, theology, and postmodernity; and Part Seven on hermeneutics, history, and theology.

2. Taking Account of a Living, Developing Tradition

This second point may admittedly at first sight seem less distinctive. Ricoeur emphasizes our dependence on a deposit of truth which is given by divine revelation, but which must *not be frozen but interpreted for today*. Many other interpreters, especially of biblical texts, have stressed this point. But here sensitivity is required. Tradition must not be substituted with some construct that some writers in the 1960s and 1970s called the "needs of modern man." That would be to replace tradition with a human-made construct where texts simply mirror the interpreter, or perhaps "anything goes." Ricoeur is robust about the need to avoid "idolatry" (in the sense of making an image of the self and venerating it). He points out that we have not yet finished with doing away the idols; man-made interpretation must be *interpretation*, not simply a new creation by the "interpreter." And that means taking interpretative tradition seriously.

On the one hand, some criterion of *continuity* must be respected; on the other hand, these diverse layers of meaning form part of Ricoeur's legitimate quest for *creative innovation*. One of the many volumes in which he especially emphasizes this is his collection of essays entitled *Essays on Biblical interpretation* (1980), edited by Lewis Mudge. Mudge writes:

> The total self-implication of the subject in such signs [i.e., words in texts under examination] is now called "testimony." Testimony generates forms of discourse which can be called revelatory. . . . We will try to show

[he continues] that this dialectic, carried out over generations, closely corresponds in the retrospective mode to Ricoeur's account of Gerhard von Rad's "tradition history" and, looking forward, to the philosopher's understanding of Jürgen Moltmann's "theology of hope."[17]

In his "Reply" to Mudge, Ricoeur emphasizes revelation and history. Discussing Hans Frei's *The Eclipse of Biblical Narrative* (1974), he writes:

> The question of the referential claims of these stories remains unavoidable. The attempt to bracket reference and to keep sense, i.e. to raise only questions of meaning and to drop questions about historical reality, fails somewhere, because it runs against my main contention that even fictions are about a world. . . . It depicts no object of the real world, but it generates an emotional model which reshapes our whole world view.[18]

Ricoeur's emphasis on *reference* and history needs to be heeded. Hans Frei's work seems to have been welcomed with acclaim in many quarters, when one might have hoped for a more critical assessment. In his book *Figuring the Sacred* (1995) Ricoeur again stresses the importance of reference and history for revelation. He has reservations about meanings that are "purely immanent to discourse."[19] He writes, "Without a doubt it is this abolition of the demonstrative or denotative characteristics of reference that makes possible the phenomenon that we call literature, where every reference to the given reality may be abolished. . . . Language seems to glorify itself without depending on the referential function of ordinary discourse."[20] The biblical text is to provide "a new world," not to rely only on the decisions of the reader.[21]

Nevertheless revelation is not "frozen." Ricoeur quotes with approval: "We too become part of an unbroken tradition

17. Ricoeur, *Essays on Biblical Interpretation*, 17.
18. Ricoeur, *Essays on Biblical Interpretation*, 44.
19. Ricoeur, *Figuring the Sacred*, 42.
20. Ricoeur, *Figuring the Sacred*, 42.
21. Ricoeur, *Figuring the Sacred*, 44.

of storytelling. Christianity is a community of storytellers."[22] Yet these stories are "traditional" and "authoritative," i.e., canonical as distinct from apocryphal ones, even if also "open" and "ongoing."[23] Again, in his essay on "The Narrative Form" (1975), Ricoeur writes of "the question of the *reference forward* to an extra-linguistic reality, *reference backward* to a speaker, and the *communication* with an audience."[24] He comments further, "The process of 'de-contextualisation' . . . opens the message to fresh interpretation according to new contexts of discourse and of life."[25]

3. Moving beyond a "Pure" or Neutral Objectivity

In any version of hermeneutics the nature of *objectivity* must be examined. Most practitioners of hermeneutics believe that "pure" objectivity has more to do with scientific precision and calculation than with hermeneutics. Ricoeur rightly argues that there is *no objectivity without subjectivity*. Hermeneutics does not follow Descartes's method of surveying the "other" or the "new" as a mere object under scrutiny by a self as subject. We saw how important this insight is for Gadamer. Ricoeur too regards this traditional Cartesian subject-object analysis as problematic.

Commenting on the phenomenology of Husserl, he writes:

> It is in the last phase of phenomenology that the critique of "objectivism" is carried to its final consequences. This critique of objectivism concerns the hermeneutical problem not only indirectly . . . but also directly because it calls into question the Diltheyan attempt to provide for the *Geisteswissenschaften* [the humanities and social sciences] a method as objective as that of the natural sciences. On the other hand, Husserl's final phenomenology joins its critique of objectivism to a positive problematic that clears the way for an ontology of understanding. This new problematic has its theme in the

22. Ricoeur, *Figuring the Sacred*, 241.

23. Ricoeur, *Figuring the Sacred*, 243.

24. Ricoeur, "Narrative Form," 68.

25. Ricoeur, "Narrative Form," 71.

Lebenswelt, the "life-world," that is a level of experience which is *anterior to the subject-object relation.*[26]

He believed that Descartes went a long way in the right direction, but he *objectified* "knowing," as David Pellauer argues.[27] He explains:

> The Cartesian subject knows itself; at least it knows itself as existing. . . . But if what a subject knows is always an object, there is a problem about its knowledge of itself. Does it know itself as an object, and hence no longer as a subject? Or is there another kind of knowing, which might be called subject knowing, which is also a kind of knowledge, but not objective knowledge? . . . Descartes already puzzled over this question.[28]

This quandary developed into the problem of selfhood discussed by Ricoeur.

Ricoeur's debt to Heidegger further ensures that any "objectivity" is not neutral. Heidegger's *Dasein* (being-there) would guarantee this. The human subject, says Heidegger, is always "situated." David Klemm shows how much this influences Ricoeur.[29] Yet, as Klemm also argues, Ricoeur's notion of the first and second naïveté represents stages of subjectivity.[30] It is in Ricoeur's discussions of Dilthey, however, that the concept of objectivity comes to the fore. This is clear in his essay, "The Task of Hermeneutics" in his *From Text to Action* (1991). He argues that the question of objectivity that persists in Dilthey's work is insoluble. Dilthey believed that "What I am for myself can only be reached through the objectifications of my own life."[31]

---

26. Ricoeur, "Existence and Hermeneutics," 8 (italics mine).

27. Pellauer, *Ricoeur,* 7–8.

28. Pellauer, *Ricoeur,* 7.

29. Klemm, *Hermeneutical Theory of Paul Ricoeur,* 31, 38.

30. Klemm, *Hermeneutical Theory of Paul Ricoeur,* 69–73. At the end of the first naïveté the self becomes objectified along the lines of Descartes, but after the second naïveté objectification is modified by phenomenology to include subjective awareness.

31. Ricoeur, *From Text to Action,* 59.

Ricoeur prefers a phenomenological approach. His rejection of "pure" objectification also emerges in his discussion of "explanation" and "understanding." As against Gadamer, he argues that we need *both* poles, not just one. The false idea of pure objectivity arises from focusing solely on explanation or descriptive causality.[32]

4. Transcending, but Not Ignoring, the Intention of the Author

Like Gadamer, Ricoeur insists that the meaning of a text often goes *beyond the immediate intention of an author*. On one side, many of us may share the view of John Calvin and others that the intention of the author remains often *a fundamental criterion of the meaning of a text*. Ricoeur defends this partly by emphasizing the importance of the human will. This emerges especially in his reservations about structuralism. Ricoeur writes, "In hermeneutics there is no closed system of the universe of signs."[33] But on the other side, the use of symbol, metaphor, and what is known as the *sensus plenior* (the fuller sense of a text) do take us beyond the author's immediate intention.

The early church found this to be the case when they searched for indirect allusions to Jesus Christ in the Old Testament. We have only to think of such biblical passages in the Old Testament as Isaiah 53 on the Suffering Servant to see that from the beginning Christian writers found passages in the Old Testament that could refer to Christ's atoning work, even if such interpretations went *beyond* the immediate or conscious horizon of the author. Ricoeur admirably makes this point in *Thinking Biblically* (1998). He writes, "The doctrine of creation is in fact inseparable from that of salvation," and appeals to Gerhard von Rad.[34] He adds, "The

32. Ricoeur, *From Text to Action*, 153; cf. 153–63.

33. Ricoeur, *Conflict of Interpretations*, 65.

34. Ricoeur and LaCocque, *Thinking Biblically*, 31.

histories recounted in Genesis 2–3 serve to universalize the description made there of the human condition."[35]

Later in the same book he considers the lamentation of Jesus drawn from Psalm 22. He writes, "The dying Jesus clothes his suffering in the words of the psalm, which he wears, so to speak, from the inside."[36] It is lamentation as prayer: "Speech had to bring to articulated expression what might have remained only cries, tears, and sighs."[37] Nevertheless, he adds, "The lament has to be set within the context of an exile, where one does not know whether it will repeat the Exodus."[38] It speaks of the abandoning of his people by God.[39] In one sense the historical context and "intention" of the psalmist must be preserved; in another sense the lamentation goes far beyond its immediate context.

We have seen the need to take the author's intention seriously but also to move well beyond the immediate intention of the text in our discussions in the previous chapter of the parables of Jesus. We have seen clearly that Jesus does not simply say, "Make anything you like of this," but on the other hand, the expositions by Geraint Vaughan Jones, John Dominic Crossan, and Dan Otto Via take us far beyond the immediate intention of Jesus through an existential hermeneutic of the parable. In *The Conflict of Interpretations*, Ricoeur declares, "Being speaks in many ways. Symbolism's raison d'être is to open the multiplicity of meaning to the equivocalness of being."[40] He comments, "To interpret is to understand a double meaning."[41]

We earlier stressed that "intention" could well be expressed in the form of an *adverb* (i.e. "intentionally") to describe an act of will that was purposively *directed toward a goal*, but not as an abstract noun as if to imply that "intention" was a "thing," or a

---

35. Ricoeur and LaCocque, *Thinking Biblically*, 33.

36. Ricoeur and LaCocque, *Thinking Biblically*, 211.

37. Ricoeur and LaCocque, *Thinking Biblically*, 215.

38. Ricoeur and LaCocque, *Thinking Biblically*, 223.

39. Ricoeur and LaCocque, *Thinking Biblically*, 224.

40. Ricoeur, *Conflict of Interpretations*, 67.

41. Ricoeur, *Conflict of Interpretations*, 8.

reified abstraction. Ricoeur makes a similar point specifically in connection with Merleau-Ponty. He says, "Only then [i.e. in the light of Husserl's phenomenology] will it be possible to recover in a non-psychological sense the notions of intentionality, outward directedness, and expression in the sense of Merleau-Ponty."[42] He has much more to clarify about intention, which we consider later under the heading on intersubjectivity and otherness.

5. Taking Full Account of Different Levels of Meaning

Ricoeur stresses different *levels of meaning* in *The Conflict of Interpretations*, in his *Freud and Philosophy*, and in his *Thinking Biblically*. I first became convinced of this point in my work on Bernard Lonergan. In his essay "The Problem of Double Meaning," as we noted, Ricoeur writes, "The dream is treated by Freud as a *narration*, which . . . has internal multiplicity."[43] First, *suspicion* is necessary because human beings still construct deceptive idols as a defence. Yet, second, *listening* is also necessary because under human utterances symbols "give rise to thought" and can convey life and revelation.[44]

In biblical interpretation, the diversity of levels of interpretation becomes immediately apparent in the traditional distinctions between allegorical interpretation, typology, and other forms of what is sometimes called the *sensus plenior*. The most striking of Ricoeur's examples come in his essay "The Nuptial Metaphor," which especially considers the Song of Solomon. He first distinguishes the rise and fall of allegorical interpretation from other ways of understanding the Song of Solomon as other or more than an erotic dialogue. He writes:

> For my part, I would like to oppose multiple, flowering history readings, set within the framework of the history

42. Ricoeur, *Conflict of Interpretations*, 253.
43. Ricoeur, *Conflict of Interpretations*, 65 (his italics).
44. Ricoeur, *Conflict of Interpretations*, 543.

of reception of the text to this unilinear conception of the "trajectory" of explication of the Song of Songs. This is a history where not just recent allegorical exegesis finds a place, but also modern scientific exegesis, and . . . new theological interpretations whether related or not to the older allegorical exegesis.[45]

All the same, there are features of the text that "hold it open to a plurality of interpretations, among which allegorical readings, which are themselves multiple and even contrary to one another, would find a place, . . . a poem with several voices that celebrates the love of a man and woman "[46] Song of Solomon 3:7–11 refers to King Solomon, so might this not be a poem about three people, "a shepherd, a shepherdess, and the king, Solomon"?[47] But these figures are "indeterminate." In 5:2 the lover says, "I am sleeping but my heart is awake." May the lover not see the King in his dreams? This might seem incomprehensible if we did not distinguish between a narrative (the narrative voice) from a poem (the poetic voice). The question "who?" is relevant to the narrative voice, but not to the poetic voice.[48] Are narrative and poetry on the same level? Ricoeur argues that much in the Song "is not said in a descriptive mode. Rather it is sung."[49]

Ricoeur now states his main concern. He writes:

> The true denouement is to be found in 8:6 ("set me like a seal on your heart, like a seal on your arm"), then what is important is not the carnal consummation, which is never described, never recounted, but the covenant vow, signified by the "seal," which is the soul of the nuptial, a soul that would have as its flesh the physical consummation that is merely sung. But when the nuptial is invested in the erotic, the flesh is soul and the soul is flesh.[50]

45. Ricoeur, "Nuptial Metaphor," 265.
46. Ricoeur, "Nuptial Metaphor," 267.
47. Ricoeur, "Nuptial Metaphor," 269.
48. Ricoeur, "Nuptial Metaphor," 270.
49. Ricoeur, "Nuptial Metaphor," 272.
50. Ricoeur, "Nuptial Metaphor," 272.

He explains that Origen and some of the church fathers used allegorical interpretation of the Song, but their pastoral insights demonstrated not the meaning of the Song, but its pastoral "use."[51] Origen also risked suggesting a two-level distinction between the material and the so-called spiritual, but this reflected Plato rather than the Bible. Allegory did not constitute the only way or the best way of discovering a "fuller" or extended meaning.

Historical-critical exegesis could bring to bear on the meaning of the Song a multitude of metaphors and images drawn from other parts of Scripture and from the historical background of the Song. Extensions of meaning can be grasped by "the weaving together of these metaphors in relation to their ultimate corporeal referent."[52] Ricoeur adds, "The poetic sublimation at the very heart of the erotic removes the need for contortions meant to de-sexualise the referent."[53] Citing the abundant references in canonical Scripture to the nuptial relation between the church and God, he refers to two major passages of Paul: Ephesians 5:25, "Husbands love your wives as Christ has loved the church," and 2 Corinthians 11:2, "for I promised you in marriage to one husband, like a pure virgin to present to Christ."[54]

Scripture, Ricoeur continues, "is a vast field of interrelated words, a unitary field, in which every word has reason and where, as a consequence, every possible linkage or comparison between words is not just authorised but even called for."[55] This is not stated in terms of a Platonic dualism, he says, and Jean Daniélou and Henri de Lubac have substantiated this point.[56] He concludes, "The language of the Song of Songs turns out to be irreplaceable. Without it, mystical experience would remain mute. That is why the 'nuptial' is a necessary recourse for such experience."[57] Ricoeur

51. Ricoeur, "Nuptial Metaphor," 277.
52. Ricoeur, "Nuptial Metaphor," 273.
53. Ricoeur, "Nuptial Metaphor," 274.
54. Ricoeur, "Nuptial Metaphor," 279.
55. Ricoeur, "Nuptial Metaphor," 283.
56. Ricoeur, "Nuptial Metaphor," 283.
57. Ricoeur, "Nuptial Metaphor," 284.

concludes by reminding us of Luther's attempt to abandon allegory. He set out faith "within the setting of the worldly location—work and marriage—[and] took away from monastic life its paradigmatic character and forbade seeing it as the privileged setting for the correct reading of the Song of Songs."[58] His final solution to other passages of Scripture concerns Gen 2:23: "This at last is bone of my bone and flesh of my flesh." This, he says, excludes the distress of something lacking, the lack of a true partner.[59] The literal text of the Song is reflected in numerous passages. The *covenant* theme is strongly present.

Initially, as I have noted, my interest in different "levels" of meaning was prompted by Bernard Lonergan. In his book *Insight*, he rejects the notion of a universal viewpoint, but clarifies meanings in terms of different levels: an experiential level, a level that depends on insight, thought, and judgment, and a cognitional level that includes an act of will.[60] Different levels of expression depend on different cognitive capacities of the human subject.[61] Philosophers of religion and philosophers of language often speak of "levels" to distinguish between empirical outlooks and aesthetic, musical, or religious outlooks. Ricoeur does not readily use the term "levels" explicitly, but certainly expresses what others mean by the term. He is careful to avoid a "Platonic" or ontological dualism.

6. Addressing Expanding Horizons, Rather Than Starting with Presuppositions

The very use of *the term "horizon"* is invaluable for exponents of hermeneutics. A horizon is always capable of *change or expansion* and moves and changes as we move. Both Hans Georg Gadamer and Wolfhart Pannenberg, as well as Ricoeur, have underlined the

58. Ricoeur, "Nuptial Metaphor," 293.
59. Ricoeur, "Nuptial Metaphor," 297.
60. Lonergan, *Insight*, 569.
61. Lonergan, *Insight*, 370–73.

importance of *expanding* horizons, in Pannenberg's case especially for theology. The term is utterly different from "presupposition." A presupposition suggests a fixed, sometimes defensive, standpoint, whereas horizon permits negotiation with a text or with someone's opinion or belief. Even more important, it allows for self-correction and advance in understanding, as listening and reading reshape our initial horizon.

The term has its origin in Husserl, a philosopher whose thought especially interested Ricoeur. Husserl wrote, "To every perception there always belongs a horizon of the past, as a potentiality of awakenable recollections; and to every recollection there belongs, as a horizon, the continuous intervening intentionality of possible recollection . . . up to the actual Now of perception."[62] In other words, while to gain complete perception would require us to be omniscient, a "horizon" can give us *potential* glimpses of something "more" than the present "now."

Heidegger, Bultmann, Fuchs, and Gadamer used the term "horizon" frequently. Heidegger writes in broad terms: "Time needs to be explicated primordially as the horizon for the understanding of being."[63] Nowadays it has become a conventional term in many other areas. In his collection of essays, *From Text to Action* (1991), Ricoeur writes:

> Wherever there is a situation, there is an *horizon* that may *contract or expand*. As the visual circle of our existence attests, the landscape is organised into the near, the far, and the open. It is the same in historical understanding. At one time it was thought that the concept of horizon could be accounted for by assimilating it to the methodological rule of placing oneself in the other's point of view: the horizon is the horizon of the other. It was thus thought that history had been aligned with the objectivity of the sciences: to adopt the other's point of view while forgetting one's own, is that not objectivity? Yet nothing

---

62. Husserl, *Cartesian Meditations*, 44–45. Saulus Genisas has recently written on the origin of the term "horizon" in Husserl with reference to potentiality and time. Genisas, *The Origin of the Horizon in Husserl's Phenomenology*.

63. Heidegger, *Being and Time*, 39.

is more disastrous than this fallacious assimilation. For the text, thus treated as an absolute object, is divested of its claim to tell us something. This claim can be sustained only by the idea of a prior understanding concerning the thing itself. . . . By restoring the dialectic of points of view and the tension between the other and the self, we arrive at the culminating concept of the fusion of horizons.[64]

7. Relating "Horizons" to Preliminary Understanding

The term *"horizon"* is bound up with another term, namely *preunderstanding* (German, *Vorverständnis*), *initial understanding*, or *preliminary understanding* in English. Ricoeur's previous observation in *From Text to Action* implicitly makes this point. Bultmann made this notion famous for a larger audience in his celebrated essay "Is Exegesis without Presuppositions Possible?" (1957). He insisted that the exegete is not a *tabula rasa* (a blank slate) but is "determined by his own individuality."[65] To understand economic history or a musical score requires some *prior* understanding of economics or music. Historical understanding requires "a relation of the interpreter to the subject."[66] Bultmann admits that "historical knowledge is never a closed or definitive knowledge."[67]

In a parallel essay, "The Problem of Hermeneutics" (1950), Bultmann asserts, "Interpretation always presupposes a living relationship to the subjects which are directly or indirectly expressed in the text."[68] One further example comes from his essay "What Does It Mean to Speak of God?" (1925) when, like Barth, he distinguishes between speech *about* God (as if to make him an "object") and speech *from* God (when God is *"subject"*

---

64. Ricoeur, *From Test to Action*, 274–75 (first italics, his; second, mine).

65. Bultmann, "Is Exegesis without Presuppositions Possible?," 349, 344.

66. Bultmann, "Is Exegesis without Presuppositions Possible?," 347

67. Bultmann, "Is Exegesis without Presuppositions Possible?," 348

68. Bultmann, "Problem of Hermeneutics," 242; cf. 234–61.

addressing us).[69] In his essay "Preface to Bultmann," Ricoeur accepts the assumptions with which Bultmann approaches the problem of interpretation. But he does not accept that the content of what Bultmann seeks to interpret is exhaustively equivalent to the interpreter's preunderstanding. The acts of God remain as important as his Word. He offers his comments as a "supplement" rather than a rejection of Bultmann's work.[70]

8. Intersubjectivity, the Self, Continuity of Identity, and "Otherness"

Ricoeur underlines a needed emphasis on *intersubjectivity*. This is clear especially in his late work *Oneself as Another* (Fr., 1990; Eng., 1992), which we shall consider in more detail than other works because of its huge importance. He begins with a reconsideration of selfhood, which had also been the theme of his earliest work, *The Voluntary and Involuntary* (1966), and his doctoral dissertation *Freedom and Nature* (published in 1966). A human person is not simply a "What," but a *"Who."* Gabriel Marcel had influenced him in adopting this emphasis. Marcel emphasized that the human being is unique, not to be reduced to a number or a case. Ricoeur stresses "a dialectic complementary to that of selfhood and of sameness, namely the dialectic of *self* and the *other than self.*"[71]

Descartes had made a valiant attempt to examine selfhood, but tended to imply a self who was more of a "what" than a "who." Further, as Dilthey had pointed out, such a self was an isolated entity, in whose veins "no real blood flowed." Ricoeur saw selfhood as dependent on God. He writes, "Left to itself, the 'I' of the cogito is Sisyphus condemned . . . to push up the rock of its certainty, fighting the slope of doubt. In contrast . . . God confers on the certainty of myself the permanence that it does not hold in itself."[72]

---

69. Bultmann, "What Does it Mean to Speak of God?," 53–65.

70. Bultmann, "What Does it Mean to Speak of God?," 72.

71. Ricoeur, *Oneself as Another*, 3.

72. Ricoeur, *Oneself as Another*, 9.

In his second essay, Ricoeur turns to those philosophers who in the tradition of P. F. Strawson hold a more complex notion of identity. Strawson's notion of combining "M" predicates (which denote material or bodily qualities) with "P" predicates (which denote personal qualities) takes us further, but not far enough.[73] In his third essay, Ricoeur sees a distinct advance in *speech-act philosophers* such as François Récanati, John Austin, and John Searle. They stress the self as *active* subject. He comments, "The illocutionary act consists in what the speaker *does in speaking*."[74] This implies a dialogical relationship with "the other," and Wittgenstein, he notes, made room for "anchorage" within the public world.[75] But even this still needs to go further. Ricoeur appeals to a wider philosophy of language.

Ricoeur's fourth essay concerns distinguishing between "cause" and "motive," in which he notes G. E. M. Anscombe's critique on Hume. This leads to a conceptual analysis of *intention*. It remains difficult to have a concept of "undeclared intention."[76] He notes Anscombe's distinction between multiple senses of intention, and Davidson's attempt in 1963 to emphasize the adverbial use of intention, *intentionally*, as I have explored above.[77] Ricoeur insists that these issues cannot be solved apart from a full concept of the human "person."

The second half of the essay concerns the problem of ascription. *Ascribing* is not describing. Ricoeur turns to the seminal work of H. L. A. Hart.[78] The aim of Hart's essay was to distinguish the ascription of responsibility from mere description. E.g., the sentence "I did it" might look like description, but in appropriate contexts it may serve as "guilty" or "I take responsibility." This is not description, but an act of judgement. Hart rightly relates this

---

73. Ricoeur, *Oneself as Another*, 27–39.

74. Ricoeur, *Oneself as Another*, 43 (Ricoeur's italics).

75. Ricoeur, *Oneself as Another*, 51.

76. Ricoeur, *Oneself as Another*, 68.

77. Ricoeur, *Oneself as Another*, 74–80.

78. Ricoeur, *Oneself as Another*, 99; and Hart, "Ascription of Responsibility and Rights."

to acts of judgment in the philosophy of law, which again demonstrates the breadth of his multidisciplinary concerns.

Ricoeur's fifth essay considers personal identity in relation to *narrative identity*. He acknowledges, "The greatest lacuna in our earlier studies most obviously concerns the temporal dimension of the self as well as of action as such."[79] Personal identity, he says, can be articulated only in the *temporal* dimension of human existence. This remains essential since many changes take place with the passing of time and without a temporal dimension we should encounter puzzles and paradoxes in the notion of personal identity. Here he also looks back consciously to his major work, *Time and Narrative*, in which he pursues this theme exhaustively. He appeals to Dilthey's notion of *the connectedness of life*.

Ricoeur again stresses that the question of "who?" cannot be reduced to the question of "what?" He insists that permanence of identity time is bound up with two issues: "*character* and *keeping one's word*."[80] Character can be seen not only in individual terms but also in corporate terms. This necessarily is seen in *habit*. A *succession of stable habits* leads to an intelligible and stable character.[81] Self-constancy, he argues, involves "keeping one's word, faithfulness to the word that has been given."[82] This self-constancy, in turn, is seen in the *act of promising*. As Ricoeur argues, David Hume's mantra, "I can never catch myself at any time without a perception" constitutes an irrelevance to the deeper question of self-identity.[83] Hume's account of perception could never make room for Ricoeur's understanding of accountability.

Ricoeur's sixth study concerns the self and *narrative identity*. Here he returns to "the interconnection of events constituted by emplotment."[84] Predictably he again appeals to Dilthey's notion of *the interconnectedness of life*. He also appeals to Gerhard von Rad's

79. Ricoeur, *Oneself as Another*, 113.

80. Ricoeur, *Oneself as Another*, 118 (Ricoeur's italics).

81. Ricoeur, *Oneself as Another*, 121.

82. Ricoeur, *Oneself as Another*, 123.

83. Ricoeur, *Oneself as Another*, 128.

84. Ricoeur, *Oneself as Another*, 140.

theme of tradition-history in the Old Testament. He discusses the structural models of Propp and Greimas in terms of their "functions." Their "actantial" [see glossary] correlation between plot, character, communication, and action is useful, but they do not pay enough attention to accountability and continuity. Ricoeur prefers to stress the interactive or intersubjective dimension.[85] He finds resonances between *Time and Narrative* and MacIntyre's *After Virtue* (1981).

This leads to the seventh study of *the self and the ethical aim*. Ricoeur considers the "good," as explored by Aristotle and MacIntyre, and "obligation" as explored by Kant. The "good" goes further than mere "obligation," although "obligation" provides an *absolute beyond the self*. Ricoeur writes, "The just, it seems to me, faces in two directions: towards the good, with respect to which it marks the extension of interpersonal relationships to institutions; and towards the legal, the judicial system [the just], conferring upon the law coherence and the right of constraint. In this study we remain exclusively on the first side of the issue."[86]

Ricoeur's eighth study concerns *the self and the moral norm*. Morally "good," as Kant insisted, means "good without qualification."[87] Ricoeur writes further, "Respect is self-esteem that has passed through the sieve of the universal and constraining norm—in short, the self-esteem under the reign of the law."[88] He draws from Heidegger his notion of "solicitude," together with the biblical maxim, "Love your neighbor as yourself" (Lev 19:18; Matt 22:39). He also expounds the ethical distinction between *"power over"* and *"power-to-do,"* which elsewhere I have also discussed with reference to Peter Geach and Gijsbert van den Brink.[89] Love and hate as subjective principles lack the universality found in

85. Ricoeur, *Oneself as Another*, 155.

86. Ricoeur, *Oneself as Another*, 197.

87. Ricoeur, *Oneself as Another*, 205.

88. Ricoeur, *Oneself as Another*, 215.

89. Ricoeur, *Oneself as Another*, 220.

THE CULMINATION OF THE APPEAL

Kant. The good life cannot be isolated but is "with and for others in just institutions."[90]

The ninth study concerns *the self and practical wisdom*. In negative terms he illustrates his ethical stance with reference to Sophocles's *Antigone*, in which confrontation leads to disruption and the tragedy of "aporia-producing limit experiences."[91] Ricoeur comments, "The fiction forged by the poet is one of conflicts which Steiner rightly considers intractable, nonnegotiable.... One of the functions of tragedy in relation to ethics is to create a gap between tragic wisdom and practical wisdom."[92] He further writes, "Hegel's philosophical project in *The Philosophy of Right* remains very close to my own views, to the extent that it reinforces the claims directed against philosophical atomism in the seventh study."[93] He stresses the difference between power and domination. Ricoeur calls for a recognition of "respect," which, we earlier noted, is one of the marks of hermeneutics as well as the use of the term "horizon." He carefully expounds the balance or dialectic between "autonomy" and dependency.[94]

Ricoeur's tenth study concerns *ontology*. As in his earlier works, he admits the importance of "attestation" or testimony. He sees the value of Heidegger's distinction between two modes of being: *Dasein* (being-there) and *Verhandenheit* (presence-at-hand).[95] Heidegger uses the two terms in a technical way: *Dasein* designates not the "what" of a human being, as if it were an object; but his or her own personal being. Heidegger's notion of "Presence-at-hand" designates in each case "possible ways for it to be."[96] Both terms avoid treating a human person as a thing or a static object. They relate to *Existenz*, not to *Sein* (Being).[97] Ricoeur

90. Ricoeur, *Oneself as Another*, 244.

91. Ricoeur, *Oneself as Another*, 243.

92. Ricoeur, *Oneself as Another*, 247.

93. Ricoeur, *Oneself as Another*, 254.

94. Ricoeur, *Oneself as Another*, 275.

95. Ricoeur, *Oneself as Another*, 309.

96. Heidegger, *Being and Time*, 67.

97. Cf. Thiselton, *Two Horizons*, 151–81.

regards these as expressing "the ontological unity of acting."[98] This, he says, relates to Aristotle's notion of *praxis*, or "the power to act."[99]

Ricoeur comments, "Aristotelian ontology invites us to look for another connection between the phenomenology of the acting and suffering self."[100] A genuine human self is *not an isolated ego*. "Otherness," Ricoeur asserts, "is not *added on to selfhood from outside*, as though to prevent its solipsistic drift, but that it belongs instead to the tenor of meaning and to the ontological constitution of selfhood is a feature that strongly distinguishes this . . . from that of selfhood and sameness."[101] He speaks of the polysemic character of otherness. To say, "I am," is to say, "I want, I move, I do."[102] "Existing is resisting"; Ricoeur chooses active, dynamic, and temporal metaphors.[103]

We have considered *Oneself as Another* more thoroughly than most other works of Ricoeur because it has led convincingly to the conclusion that intersubjectivity, personal identity, continuity, and otherness, which are vital for a living hermeneutics, raise ethical questions about accountability and institutions. This reveals the heart of Ricoeur's most distinctive contribution.

9. Narrative Theory and Its Relation to Time

In his magisterial three-volume work, *Time and Narrative* (1983–85), Ricoeur tells us that his reading of Dilthey, Aristotle, and Augustine provided the groundwork for much of his thought. Dilthey rightly saw the need for both *explanation and understanding* (German, *Erklärung und Verstehen*)—or, as Apel calls it, the E-V debate—but within the framework of time. Time also emerged

98. Ricoeur, *Oneself as Another*, 310.
99. Ricoeur, *Oneself as Another*, 312.
100. Ricoeur, *Oneself as Another*, 315.
101. Ricoeur, *Oneself as Another*, 317 (my italics).
102. Ricoeur, *Oneself as Another*, 321.
103. Ricoeur, *Oneself as Another*, 322; cf. 328.

as an essential theme in dialogue with Heidegger and Greimas. Heidegger had explored temporality (German, *Zeitlichkeit*), the transcendent ground for the possibility of time. Ricoeur learned from Heidegger the a priori nature of time. This both agrees with Dilthey and also goes beyond him. These earlier concepts of time needed correction, however; for the significance of history and tradition need development in the light of Gerhard von Rad's work on the Old Testament.

Despite the insights of Greimas, Ricoeur has deep reservations about *structuralism in relation to narrative*. He comments, "In hermeneutics there is no closed system of the universe of signs. While linguistics moves inside the enclosure of a self-sufficient universe and encounters only intrasignificant relations, . . . hermeneutics is ruled by the open state of the universe of signs."[104] He illustrates the self-governing system of linguistics from the "field semantics" of Jost Trier.[105] He adds, "From the outset this discipline adopts the axiom of the closed state of the linguistic universe."[106] This indicates, he says, the relation between the science of language (linguistics) and the philosophy of language (hermeneutics).[107] Ricoeur writes in response, as already noted, "In hermeneutics there is no closed system of the universe of signs."[108] I have repeated this point to emphasize it, and would express my deep disappointment with successive editions of the journal *Semeia*. One benefit of so-called post-structuralism is that it has unmasked the dogmatic universalism of earlier "binary" structuralism.

In volume 1 of *Time and Narrative*, Ricoeur looks at Book 11 of Augustine's *Confessions* to consider an *extension of time as past, present, and future*. Ricoeur calls this *"discordance."* Augustine regards the experience of futurity in terms of expectation; present experience is a matter of attention; past experience becomes a matter of memory. Ricoeur writes, "Through the

---

104. Ricoeur, *Conflict of Interpretations*, 65.

105. Ricoeur, *Conflict of Interpretations*, 69.

106. Ricoeur, *Conflict of Interpretations*, 73.

107. Ricoeur, *Conflict of Interpretations*, 73.

108. Ricoeur, *Conflict of Interpretations*, 65.

experience of human time (memory, attention, and hope) we come to understand the world, its objects, and our own present."[109] Quoting Augustine, he comments, "The mind 'performs three functions: expectation, . . . attention, . . . and memory.'"[110] The mind is "stretched" in these three directions. Yet Augustine does not adequately consider their interaction; he is primarily considering the contrast between time and eternity and world-history. Augustine rightly confesses, "You are the Maker of all time" (*Confessions* 13.15).[111]

To understand the logic of emplotment Ricoeur turns to Aristotle. He writes in chapter 2: "Aristotle discerns in the poetic act . . . the triumph of concordance over discordance."[112] The combination of Augustine on discordance and Aristotle on concordance relates time and emplotment to human lived experience (*Erlebnis*). Ricoeur sees Augustine's notion of time as "stretched out" into past (in memory), present (which claims attention), and future (which brings expectation). This "stretching out" in time constitutes discordance. On the other hand, Aristotle brings this discordance into concordance by means of plot. In this way Augustine and Aristotle are complementary while on their own they are inadequate. Aristotle offers insights but fails to allow for temporality adequately. What he gives us is "the organization of events," in the active sense of "[o]rganizing the events into a system."[113] What we need to remedy this, according to Ricoeur, is an understanding of narrative and the role of plot. The term "poetic" expresses the dynamic aspect of emplotment. From this perspective we can understand "persons engaged in action."[114] Ricoeur considers the variety of particularities in emplotment, and

---

109. Ricoeur, *Time and Narrative*, 1:16.

110. Ricoeur, *Time and Narrative*, 1:19.

111. Cf. Augustine, *Confessions* 11.30:40 to the end; and Plato, *Timaeus* 38d.

112. Ricoeur, *Time and Narrative*, 1:31. By "poetic act" (*poēsis*) Aristotle generally means the composing of literary texts.

113. Ricoeur, *Time and Narrative*, 1:33.

114. Ricoeur, *Time and Narrative*, 1:35; and Aristotle, *Poetics* 48a1.

"configuration, imitation, or representation, in the organization of events."[115]

- *Emplotment*: many suggest that a verbal form (emplotment) coveys "plot" better than a static noun. It conveys the making of a plot in narrative.

- *Configuration*: in Ricoeur's theory, pre-narrative lived experience provoke the configuration of a narrative text-world that is inhabited by reading, and the effects spill out into the everyday world, having a decisive impact upon the identity and perspective of the reader.

- *Imitation*: for "imitation" Ricoeur often uses the term "mimesis." But this is used in more than one way. One kind of imitation is derived from lived experience, but another is derived from the narrative-world, and a third from the art of reading and understanding.

- *Representation*: in Ricoeur, representation is how we interpret reality and re-display it to ourselves. It can be applied to all sorts of cultural products and actions.

It is important that in relation to story "*The Poetics* [of Aristotle] does not speak of structure but of structuration. Structuration is an orientated activity that is only completed in the spectator (for theatre) or the reader (for literature)."[116] Most of all, "The work deploys a world that the reader appropriates."[117]

In chapter 3, Ricoeur expounds many of the consequences of his earlier consideration of discordance and concordance in Augustine and Aristotle. He writes, "The highlighting of the dynamic of emplotment is to me the key to the problem of the relation between time and narrative."[118] Again, "reception theory" is prominent. He writes, "What is at stake is the concrete process by which textual configuration mediates between the prefiguration of the practical field and its refiguration through the reception of the

115. Ricoeur, *Time and Narrative*, 1:45.

116. Ricoeur, *Time and Narrative*, 1:49.

117. Ricoeur, *Time and Narrative*, 1:50.

118. Ricoeur, *Time and Narrative*, 1:53.

work."[119] The composition of the plot, he insists, is grounded in a preunderstanding of the world of action.[120] At this point he alludes to the theory of narrative and action "in the sense given to this term by English-language analytic philosophy."[121] He also refers to Clifford Geertz on public culture and symbolic systems, and again to Heidegger's concept of temporality and historicity or historical givenness and finitude.[122]

Ricoeur expounds some of the particularities of plot, for example, of reversals in apocalyptic, and the correspondence of beginning and end. He argues that received paradigms structure readers' expectations.[123] Personally, I have regularly called attention to readers' expectations, especially in my work on Hans Robert Jauss.[124] Perhaps predictably "horizon" and "world" feature in the remainder of chapter 3, together with narrativity, reference, and time. Part 2 of this first volume of *Time and Narrative* brings us to a further point of affinity between Ricoeur and my case for hermeneutics.

10. The Distinctiveness of Fictional Narratives

In biblical hermeneutics the parables of Jesus are usually fictional stories, even if some also reflect certain historical events. Ricoeur has a strong interest in *fiction*, as well as its relation to history and historical narrative, as can be seen in his *Time and Narrative*. In his volume 2 Ricoeur considers *fictional narrative*, turning in volume 3 more explicitly to issues of history. He considers Gerard Genette's analysis of order, duration, frequency, flashbacks, and flash-forwards (or *prolepses*). These literary devices show that chronological report differs between many narratives. In the New

119. Ricoeur, *Time and Narrative*, 1:53.

120. Ricoeur, *Time and Narrative*, 1:54.

121. Ricoeur, *Time and Narrative*, 1:55.

122. Ricoeur, *Time and Narrative*, 1:58–64.

123. Ricoeur, *Time and Narrative*, 1:76.

124. Thiselton, "Reception History, H. R. Jauss, and the Formative Power of Scripture."

Testament, for example, the sequence of the temptations of Jesus, and the chronological differences relating to the cleansing of the temple, constitute classic examples.

The more important point, however, is that in Ricoeur's judgment *hermeneutics relates to the possible*, and that *fiction* often functions to *explore the possible*. Imagined possibilities can provoke the mind into thought. This may be one reason why Ricoeur has less reservation about the term *myth* than some might do; for myth, as Vanhoozer comments, "speaks of general possibilities."[125] I have explored this, not least with reference to the parables of Jesus and visual visions in the Book of Revelation in *The Power of Pictures in Christian Thought: The Use and Abuse of Images in the Bible and Theology* (2018).

Ricoeur does not detach narrative from history, as might be the case in many structuralist approaches. But he recognizes the force of Aristotle's maxim, "The distinction between historian and poet . . . consists in this, that the one describes the thing that has been, and the other a kind of thing that might be. Hence poetry is something more philosophic and of graver import than history, since its statements are of the nature rather of universals, whereas those of history are singulars."[126] All the same, Ricoeur recognizes the crucial place of history, in spite of "games with time" in literature.[127] Often a given narrative in literature "has its own system of tenses," as well as changes in the speed of time to serve a plot.[128] Moreover, often the narrator may be just as fictive as the characters in the narrative-world. A narrator may push some aspects into the background, while other aspects assume a place in the foreground.[129]

Changes of tempo are a regular feature of narratives, and I have regularly illustrated this with reference to the Gospel of Mark: up to Mark 8 events occur at a high speed, often introduced

125. Vanhoozer, *Biblical Narrative in the Philosophy of Paul Ricoeur*, 238.

126. Aristotle, *Poetics* 1451b 1–7.

127. Ricoeur, *Time and Narrative*, 2:61–99.

128. Ricoeur, *Time and Narrative*, 2:63.

129. Ricoeur, *Time and Narrative*, 2:70–71.

with the Greek word *euthus,* meaning, almost, "immediately"; the central chapters proceed at normal speed; the Passion narrative is in slow motion. The whole scheme places weight on the centrality of the cross and Passion week.[130]

Ricoeur considers narrated time and various relations between time and narrative in such authors as Gerard Genette, and in the second section of volume 2 of *Time and Narrative* considers such narrative devices as "point of view" and "narrative voice."[131] The narrative category of "point of view" constitutes a fundamental tool of hermeneutics, which I have discussed in various studies. Perhaps most prominent of all is my appeal to the narrative theory of Robert Alter in using "point of view" to explain the perspective of those narratives that have sometimes been dismissed as "doublets" or mere clumsy duplication of the same basic story from different sources.[132] For example, to a hasty reader it may seem as if there are two contradictory accounts of the call of David in 1 Samuel 16:1–23 and 1 Samuel 17:1—2 Samuel 5:5 respectively. Alter interprets these two narratives as representing stereoscopic perspectives, one from "the point of view" of divine control (1 Sam 16:12–13) and the other from "the point of view" of "the hurly-burly of human life "(1 Sam 17:1—2 Sam 5:5).

I have similarly cited Mikhail Bakhtin and his work on Dostoevsky on the concept of polyphonic and dialogic narration (in contrast to monologic narration) in such sources as the Book of Job. Sometimes a profound truth is too complex to be expressed fully by a single voice.[133] Bakhtin comments:

> *A plurality of independent and unknown voices and consciousnesses, a genuine polyphonic of fully valid voices is in fact the chief characteristic of Dostoevsky's novels.*

130. Ricoeur, *Time and Narrative*, 2:72-77, with reference to Herald Weinrich.

131. Ricoeur, *Time and Narrative*, 2:88-99.

132. Alter, *Art of Biblical Narrative*, 147-53.

133. Cf. Clark and Holquist, *Mikhail Bakhtin*; Morson and Emerson, *Mikhail Bakhtin*; and Bakhtin, *Problems of Dostoevsky's Poetics*, 5-46 and throughout.

What unfolds in his works is not [only] a multitude of
characters in a single objective world, illuminated by
a single authorial consciousness; but rather, [Bakhtin
suggests], *a plurality of consciousnesses with equal rights
and each with its own world*, combine, but are not
merged, in the unity of the event.[134]

11. The Role of History and of Historical External Reference

In volume 3 of *Time and Narrative* Ricoeur introduces the subject of history by considering Husserl's approach to time.[135] Husserl speaks of "the temporally creative acts of the now and the
past."[136] Kant, as is well-known, ascribed time, as well as space and
causal agencies to "inner" categories imposed by the human mind.
Ricoeur, however, argues that Kant failed to take account of the
double experience of time as both human time and clock time.
Ricoeur next compares the earlier and later writings of Heidegger.
He does not want readers to discount Heidegger's earlier emphasis
on the human experience of time (or lived time), even if he also
recognizes its unfinished character.[137]

Chronology is not necessarily the most important thing
about history. Cosmological, astronomical, or chronological time
that clocks or the solar system measure is not the closest to human experience. Vanhoozer writes, "The 'end' is not simply the
last thing to happen in a sequence, but the conclusion of a story.
The conclusion 'follows' neither chronologically nor logically from
what has gone before, but rather teleologically."[138] Ricoeur wishes
to retain Heidegger's notion of making possible, or potentiality
and futurity.[139] He also considers critically Heidegger's notion of

134. Bakhtin, *Problems of Dostoevsky's Poetics*, 6 (his italics).

135. Ricoeur, *Time and Narrative*, 3:23–44.

136. Ricoeur, *Time and Narrative*, 3:33.

137. Ricoeur, *Time and Narrative*, 3:60–61.

138. Vanhoozer, *Biblical Narrative*, 93.

139. Ricoeur, *Time and Narrative*, 3:70.

historical finitude or historicality, and its relation to "care" and "preoccupation."[140]

Ricoeur concludes that his goal is to formulate the refiguration of time "through the interweaving of history and fiction."[141] He does not find an entirely "objective" view of history satisfactory, but all the same insists that in the biblical tradition there is an interweaving of narrative and kerygma. He wants to preserve the indissolubility of the Jesus of history and the Christ of faith. The life of Jesus, he says, is a life to which there is testimony. Jesus's work is the announcement of a new age. The message of Jesus sets in motion not simply a new vision, but a "vision of the world that is never ethically neutral, but that implicitly or explicitly induces an evaluation of the world and of the reader as well."[142] The Word, says John, was made flesh. Despite the complexities of the term "real," the "re-enactment of the past in the present" does depend on a reappropriation of events in history.[143] Yet "history" is "the enactment of past thought in the historian's own mind."[144]

The Christian sacraments are often described as a "making contemporary" of past events. But the past events in question are historically definite. In his essay on "The Narrative Form" Ricoeur endorses "the question of the reference forward to an extra-linguistic reality, the reference backward to a speaker, and the communication with an audience."[145] These three aspects together constitute an "event" in the discourse. We have stressed the importance of historical events for Ricoeur in our second point about a living, developing tradition, especially in revelation.

140. Ricoeur, *Time and Narrative*, 3:80–96.

141. Ricoeur, *Time and Narrative*, 3:180.

142. Ricoeur, *Time and Narrative*, 3:249.

143. Ricoeur, *Time and Narrative*, 3:144.

144. Ricoeur, *Time and Narrative*, 3:145.

145. Ricoeur, "Narrative Form," 66.

12. The Types and Functions of Metaphor and Symbol

We have already considered much of Ricoeur's work on metaphor above, especially under point 5, on levels of meaning, and also in section 3 of chapter 3. In his books *The Rule of Metaphor* and *Interpretation Theory*, he considers the many functions that metaphor performs. In the latter book he speaks of the symbol as "the surplus of meaning."[146] On the theory of metaphor he writes, "The relation between the literal meaning and the figurative meaning in a metaphor is like an abridged version within a single sentence of the complex interplay of significations that characterise the literary work as a whole."[147] He adds, "What a poem states is related to what it suggests just as its primary signification is related to its secondary signification where both significations fall within the semantic field. . . . It is a positive and productive use of ambiguity."[148]

Further, metaphor shifts to the semantics of *the sentence* what was previously the semantics of the *word*. Ricoeur comments, "Metaphor is a trope. . . . It represents the extension of the meaning of the name through deviation from the literal meaning of words."[149] Here he refers to Max Black, Philip Wheelwright, and others. Further, he says:

> It is the conflict between these two interpretations that sustains metaphor. . . . Thus metaphor does not exist in itself, but in and through interpretation. The metaphorical interpretation presupposes a literal interpretation which becomes self-destructive in a significant contradiction. It is this process of self-destruction or transformation which imposes a sort of twist on the words, an extension of meaning thanks to which we can make sense where a literal interpretation would be literally nonsensical.[150]

146. Ricoeur, *Interpretation Theory*, 45.
147. Ricoeur, *Interpretation Theory*, 46.
148. Ricoeur, *Interpretation Theory*, 47.
149. Ricoeur, *Interpretation Theory*, 49.
150. Ricoeur, *Interpretation Theory*, 50.

Ricoeur compares the function of metaphors to what Gilbert Ryle called a category mistake, but in metaphor it is a calculated error. A tension is set up between the metaphor and its literal meaning. Dead metaphors such as "the foot of a chair" do not show this tension, but live metaphors work only where such tension or contradiction exists. He argues that both metaphors and symbols operate with "double meaning," as we have observed, and as Freud indicated about layers of dreams.[151]

A symbol, therefore, works "as the model for the extension of meaning," and functions as a "surplus of signification."[152] Further, he says, "The interplay of similarity and dissimilarity presents, in effect, the conflict between some prior categorisation of reality and the new one just being born."[153] He adds, "A symbol cannot be exhaustively treated by conceptual language, but there is more in a symbol than in any of its conceptual equivalents."[154] The functions of a symbol and a metaphor are almost infinite. There is no given categorisation, he argues, that can "embrace all the semantic possibilities of a symbol."[155]

Ricoeur also argues that the time-bound character of symbols makes all the difference between symbol and metaphor: "The latter is a free invention discourse; the former is bound to the cosmos."[156] Ricoeur is drawing on the supposedly natural basis of genuine symbols, whereas metaphors can be coined at will. Hence, "In this sense a minimal hermeneutic is required for the functioning of any symbolism."[157] What Ricoeur calls "root metaphors" are often indistinguishable from symbolic paradigms. They have the power to bring two separate domains "into cognitive and emotional relation by using language directly appropriate for the

151. Ricoeur, *Interpretation Theory*, 53.
152. Ricoeur, *Interpretation Theory*, 55.
153. Ricoeur, *Interpretation Theory*, 56.
154. Ricoeur, *Interpretation Theory*, 57.
155. Ricoeur, *Interpretation Theory*, 57.
156. Ricoeur, *Interpretation Theory*, 6.
157. Ricoeur, *Interpretation Theory*, 63.

one as a lens of seeing the other."[158] He adds, "Metaphor implies a tensive use of language in order to uphold an intensive concept of reality."[159] Thus, the multiform character of metaphors is evidence of their many forms and diverse functions.

I have addressed these issues myself in numerous places throughout my career, most recently in *The Power of Pictures in Christian Thought: The Use and Abuse of Images in the Bible and Theology* (2018).

13. Appropriation and Distance in Hermeneutics

There are at least two ways of understanding *distance*. In *Interpretation Theory*, Ricoeur speaks of "the dialectic of distanciation and appropriation" (see glossary).[160] To appropriate a meaning, he says, "is to make [it] 'one's own.'"[161] In this context, "distance" denotes "the actual spatial and temporal gap between us and . . . [the] work of art or discourse" and its "otherness."[162] We need to overcome a cultural estrangement. This is reflected in my definition of hermeneutics as "how we read, understand, and handle texts, especially those written in another time or in a context of life different from our own."[163]

There is a second sense in which there is a need for "distance" in hermeneutics. Ricoeur admits that "distanciation" can be used in several ways, including "distanciation of self from itself within the interior of appropriation. This distanciation implements all the strategies of suspicion. . . . Distanciation in all its forms and figures constitutes par excellence the critical moment in understanding."[164] This might be said to mark the distinction between interpretation and hermeneutics as the second-order critical reflection on the

158. Ricoeur, *Interpretation Theory*, 67.

159. Ricoeur, *Interpretation Theory*, 68.

160. Ricoeur, *Interpretation Theory*, 44.

161. Ricoeur, *Interpretation Theory*, 43.

162. Ricoeur, *Interpretation Theory*, 43.

163. Thiselton, *Hermeneutics*, 1.

164. Ricoeur, *From Text to Action*, 35.

very nature of interpretation and understanding, including the criteria for its validity.

In a much wider sense this notion of distanciation and appropriation may also partly reflect the mediaeval practice that was often known as *Lectio Divina*. This way of reading the Bible is associated with Gregory I, Benedict, and the Dominican Order, and was re-emphasized by John of the Cross and later Vatican II. *Lectio Divina* is a "ladder" of four steps: first, reading the biblical text (*lectio*); second, meditation or reflection on it (*meditatio*); third, prayer for self-involvement and commitment (*oratio*); and fourth, contemplation especially of the glory of God (*contemplatio*). Ricoeur, as a Protestant, does not allude, to my knowledge, explicitly to *Lectio Divina*, but his dialectic between a hermeneutic of suspicion and appropriation constitutes at least a close parallel with it. For example, in his *Thinking Biblically* he discusses the universal meaning of the fall in Genesis 3 with reference to Col 1:15, "He [Christ] is before all things."[165]

These thirteen points in the thought of Ricoeur do not exhaust this appeal but are enough to indicate where this case for hermeneutics finds its culmination as well as clear parallels in the thought of Ricoeur. It is hardly necessary to say that I heartily endorse all of these points, and indeed have affirmed them in my previous books, even if not always with explicit reference to Ricoeur.

Should it seem to be unrealistic to express such unqualified approval of Ricoeur, this does not mean that I have no queries whatever. I tentatively wonder whether his advocacy of the very wide scope for diversity in interpretation should not have been a little more cautious. Nevertheless, he emphasizes the place of revelation, covenant, and tradition in biblical studies, as well as the danger of idolatry. He implicitly qualifies his defence of pluralism by stating that pluralism cannot be applied to *all kinds of texts and all kinds of readers*. His suspicion of totalitarianism and dogmatism is understandable and necessary.

Ricoeur is always generous to other views, even to those with which he has some reservations. Above all, he has shown that

165. Ricoeur, *Thinking Biblically*, 60–61.

hermeneutics promotes mutual understanding, and sometimes even reconciliation. His arguments for the universality of hermeneutics seem to surpass even Betti's. With Ricoeur, hermeneutics becomes not simply an obligation, but a joyous advance in understanding the other, whether "the other" is an alien text or another person.

Glossary of Fifty
Technical Terms

Actantial models are closely associated with Alexander J. Greimas (1966 and 1970) in his structural approach to narrative in which he analyses different *actors, actions,* and *roles* within a story. He distinguished, for example, broadly between subject and object, but also more specifically between hero and opponent, helper and task, and so on.

Allegory differs from parable. A parable is a *coherent story* or picture in which its application is carried over to another level of reality *as a whole.* An allegory often has a *string of independent applications and evaluations.* An allegory *presupposes* an understanding; a parable *prepares for* understanding. In an allegory the audience already knows the meaning of the separate pictures, which it translates as if in a code. In a parable the audience may be caught off guard while the picture or story as a whole lifts them to a new understanding of reality. A parable is used to reconcile opposition. Allegory cannot be understood unless we know the state of affairs to which it refers. In Ezekiel 17:1–10, for example, an allegory speaks of an eagle but means the king of Babylon; it speaks of a twig of cedar but means the king of Judah. Many allegories occur in John Bunyan's *A Pilgrim's Progress.* In the house of the Interpreter Bunyan speaks of oil but means the Holy Spirit. By contrast when Jesus speaks of a woman cleaning her house, he means a real woman cleaning a real house (Luke 15:8–10), or a real younger son leaving his home (15:11–32). We are not meant to interpret the details separately. Often the parable is imprecise and "open," leaving the reader to interpret it; the allegory is precise and "closed."

Aporia is simply a philosophical term borrowed from ancient Greek to denote an impasse or insurmountable puzzle.

Code. A code provides the framework within which signs or words make sense as a piece of communication. A code is the set of conventions that constitute this frame. Communication takes place when the author or creator of a text or utterance shares the same code as the hearer, reader, or interpreter. Use of the code limits the possible scope or range of interpretation. It may prevent confusion between the everyday world and fiction, and between literal and metaphorical meaning. Umberto Eco has emphasized the importance of the code.

Concordance and **discordance** simply mean respectively harmony, accord, and agreement, and conflict, dissent, and disharmony. But Ricoeur uses the terms in a special way for narratives. He regards Augustine as promoting a notion of extended time as past, present, and future. This then corresponds with *memory* of the past, *attention* to the present, and *expectation* of the future. The "stretching out" of time constitutes its "discordance". By contrast from Aristotle he draws the "concordance" of "employment" as a single, coherent, meaningful, and harmonious notion of a unified time.

Condensation and displacement. Freud used these two terms to indicate that when the dream-as-dreamed (the dream thoughts) is recounted the account may become "brief, meagre, and laconic" and in displacement reflect sequences that may become distorted or "scrambled" by the repression of the censor, which disguises the meaning. This "overdetermination" (see later) calls for interpretation.

Critical Theory is a term coined by Max Horkheimer for the work of the Frankfurt School. This school both attacks positivism (see later) yet claims to follow scientific method and also, broadly,

Marxism. It aims at the liberation of the socially oppressed and is suspicious of totalitarianism. Critical theory in taught courses includes not only such thinkers as Gadamer and Habermas, but especially liberation hermeneutics. It includes philosophy, politics, and literature.

Differend was used by Jean-François Lyotard to denote a rationally unresolvable dispute between two opposing views. Lyotard argued that rhetoric could provide only the appearance of resolution. In Lyotard's view rhetoric substitutes for rationality, where the "stronger" rhetoric dictates the rules of the encounter.

Distanciation denotes stepping back, or distancing the observer.

Divination was used by Schleiermacher to denote the intuitive or "feminine" capacity in hermeneutics to perceive the whole or personal dimension of interpretation.

Enlightenment, the. Immanuel Kant (1724–1804) coined the term to denote humankind's liberation from learning from tutors or secondhand authorities, to the freedom to think for oneself. But many regard its origins as earlier in England, from the Deists and Hume onwards.

Extra-linguistic means that which belongs to the real world outside language, in contrast to language that merely refers to other language.

Fictional texts, according to Paul Ricoeur, have the capacity to stimulate the imagination by projecting possible (not actual) states of affairs.

Geisteswissenschaften is the German word broadly denoting the Humanities, sometimes including also the social sciences. It includes such areas as history, philosophy, theology, linguistics, and languages, like a British Faculty of Arts. It excludes the sciences. Dilthey made much of the term.

Grand narratives offer a comprehensive account of history and knowledge in contrast to the claim by postmodernists (especially Lyotard) that the plurality of the world and life prohibits them.

Such comprehensive accounts include those offered by Karl Marx and Sigmund Freud.

Handbook (engineering or transmissive) culture denotes a "closed" communicative act, i.e., one that allows no ambiguity of meaning. Directions or instructions are typical of handbook or engineering cultures or codes.

Hermeneutics denotes the theories and the art of interpretation. It is applied to written texts and sometimes to social institutions that belong to another time or culture. Its main exponents were Schleiermacher (1768–1834), Dilthey (1833–1911), Heidegger (1889–1976), Gadamer (1900–2002), and Ricoeur (1913–2005).

Heteronomy is an action that is influenced by some external force, i.e., governed under the sway of another, rather than from within. In Kant, obligation, moral law, and duty, constitute examples of moral law external to the human subject.

Historical reason derives from Georg Hegel (1770–1832), who regarded the rationalism of Leibniz, the empiricism of Locke and Hume, and the critical philosophy of Kant as lacking a necessary historical conditioning. Knowledge can be assessed, he argued, only when we consider it in its historical situation.

Historicality (sometimes also historicity) denotes the way in which knowledge is radically conditioned by its place in history. Heidegger regarded this as an important principle.

Horizon denotes not a fixed position (like presupposition), but a viewpoint that moves in accordance with the viewer. It expands as we move and is capable of very large expansion. Most major exponents of hermeneutics use the term regularly.

Incommensurability. This term has been imported into hermeneutics from the philosophy of science and is not always used accurately. Popularly it is used to denote two different views that cannot be reconciled. However, it is not quite as harsh as Lyotard's "the Differend." In the philosophy of science it may mean apparently conflicting theories that belong to different universes of discourse.

Intersubjectivity has been used in philosophy, social science, and psychology to contrast individualism or solipsism. It often denotes the corporate basis of knowledge.

Lifeworld has four uses or applications. In Wilhelm Dilthey (1833–1911) the term emphasizes the historical, living, dynamic, character of human life and institutions. More important, in Edmund Husserl (1859–1938) and his phenomenology, the term denotes human perceptions and experience allegedly logically prior to the separation of subject and object. In Jürgen Habermas (b. 1929) the term stands beside "system," where Habermas emphasizes the need for both the subject's lifeworld and a more objective system. A fourth use is among sociologists, who see lifeworld as a reality constructed by human minds in the tradition of social construction.

Metacriticism is strictly criticism of criticism but in practice seeks the *basis* for any kind of critical thinking. It contrasts with the purely pragmatic or descriptive.

Metaphor draws on ordinary language to extend its established and conventional meaning by symbol or analogy to express more than "literal" language could convey. It brings two separate domains into relation by using one domain as a lens for seeing the other. Paul Ricoeur (1913–2005) sees this interactive understanding as a creative tool of language.

Model reader is used by Eco to denote a reader who shares a code (see earlier) selected by a speaker or author to enable unambiguous communication.

Monologic and **dialogic** form a contrast that arises largely but not exclusively from Mikhail Bakhtin (1895–1938), the Russian literary critic, philosopher, and specialist in semiotics. Working especially on Dostoevsky, he developed the Socratic notion of the dialogic nature of truth as that which is born out of dialogue between people. Monologic discourse, he urged, states only ready-made, premature, inadequate thought. Truth is too great and too complex to be limited to a single parson's thought. In Dostoevsky's

The Brothers Karamazov, truth is conveyed by all three different brothers, not by a single voice, just as in the book of Job, where truth is conveyed by the conversations between God, Satan, Job, and Job's four friends. The book of Job conveys its complex message concerning suffering through dialogic discourse.

Narrative worlds. Narratives project "worlds" to be entered by readers, and narrative worlds offer unique advantages in hermeneutics. Readers today enter narrative worlds almost every day through television, soap operas, and fiction. Narratives create "worlds" in which readers participate. Jesus created such worlds in many of his parables. These were self-consistent in their details, unlike allegories (see earlier). In the narrative world prejudices or resistances may become weaker, as a reader comes to grasp a new reality.

Objectification denotes turning any phenomenon into a passive object of scrutiny. Descartes is accused of objectifying the self by making it an object of scrutiny. Phenomenology attempts to reach behind this objectification to a perception that is prior to the dualism of subject and object. Critics of phenomenology doubt whether this is logically possible.

Open and closed texts. Usually "closed" texts encourage a particular interpretation, while "open" texts encourage multiple interpretations. In Eco's work, typically closed texts are "engineering" texts, designed to transmit information. Road signs offer another example. At the opposite end of a spectrum poetry often offers the most open texts, where various layers of meaning may be suggested. But there are intermediate positions. Some suggest that often the Pauline epistles are more closed than many parables in the Gospels. In the case of flood warnings, a closed communication may specify danger at a given height; an open warning may speak of the water level, while leaving the reader to judge what level constitutes a danger.

Otherness at its simplest simply denotes difference. But many sociologists relate the term to self-identity and emphasize feelings of not belonging, as may be experienced within minority or marginalized groups, and so on. Encounters with otherness often means encountering people who are different in race, gender, or class.

Overdetermination arises from double-layered or multilayered texts. Interpretation aims at resolving such ambiguity. It occurs when a single observed fact is determined by multiple cause, one of which would be sufficient to account for (or determine) the effect.

Perspectivalism arises from the claim that two views, which otherwise appear contradictory, can both be true from different perspectives. John Locke (1632–1704) suggested that such qualities as colors, sounds, and tastes are not objectively given but are interpreted differently by different minds. Johann Chladenius (1710–59) expounded the idea of "a point of view" or perspective in hermeneutics from which two accounts of the same object might arise. Ludwig Wittgenstein (1889–1970) applied Jastrow's example of a duck-rabbit to the same effect. Jastrow's drawing can be seen as a rabbit's head looking upwards or as a duck's beak looking to the left. Donald Evans (in 1963) developed "seeing . . . as" as providing different "onlooks" within a system.

Phenomenology arises from reflection, especially on consciousness, which is allegedly logically prior to the objectification (i.e., making an object of thought) of consciousness and avoids a subject-object split by observing phenomena without objectifying them. It is associated with Edmund Husserl (1859–1938), but also with Marcel, Merleau-Ponty, and often Ricoeur. Husserl argued that we may perceive "essences" only if our assumptions about the world are bracketed or suspended. This "bracketing" may account for controversy with critics, who claim that the aim is logically impossible. It is distinctively a German-French philosophical tradition. Some describe it as not a doctrine, but a style of thought.

Polysemy is the capacity of a sign (word, phrase, or symbol) to have more than one meaning (from Greek, *pola*, many, and *semeia*, signs).

Positivism denotes the view that restricts reality to what is evidential, empirical, observational, and material. Sometimes it confuses scientific method with a mechanistic worldview. It is often associated with Auguste Comte (1798–1857). Some describe Logical Positivism (associated with A. J. Ayer) as positivism in linguistic dress.

Postmodernism. At its best, postmodernism protests against the standardization of all knowledge according to positivism or the Enlightenment, which privileges scientific method as the model for all knowledge. At its worst it signifies a radical and unresolvable pluralism in logic, in religion, and in culture. The extreme example is Jean-François Lyotard (1924–98) and his notion of the Differend, which declared that it is impossible to arbitrate rationally between two opposing views. European postmodernism is associated with Michel Foucault (1926–84) and Jacques Derrida (1930–2004); American postmodernism, with Richard Rorty (1931–2007) and Stanley Fish (b. 1938). They regard the truth of literary texts as being entirely relative to readers.

Preunderstanding is an overliteral translation of the German word *Vorverständnis*. This has become a technical term following its widespread use in Dilthey, Heidegger, and Bultmann. It could have been translated into more idiomatic English as "preliminary understanding." For it simply means a first step towards understanding. Bultmann illustrates this in terms of musical or mathematical texts. A general understanding of music or mathematics provides a "preunderstanding" of musical or mathematical texts.

Rationalism stresses the role of reason in knowing. It is one of the three classical traditions in philosophy, the other two being empiricism and critical or Kantian philosophy. Its classical exponents were Leibniz, Descartes, and Spinoza (in contrast to the empiricists Locke, Berkeley, and Hume). However, Hegel expounded a historical rationalism.

Reader-response theories take various forms, but they all call attention to the active role of communities of readers in constructing what counts for them as "what the text means." The classic exponent of reader-response theories is Wolfgang Iser (1926–2007). He drew on a theory of perception to establish the active and participatory role of readers in "filling in" or completing a textual meaning that would otherwise remain only potential. Readers actualize this meaning. Iser draws on Roman Ingarden and Husserl. We see a table, for example, as having four legs, although only three can actually be seen, and we "fill out" what is assumed. We construe what we see. Iser applied this to literary texts. The readers fill in the blanks. Umberto Eco goes a little further; Holland and Bleich go much further. Finally Stanley Fish (b. 1938), combining it with postmodernism, applied this much more radically, and reader-response becomes a matter of the readers' creation of meaning.

Referential. A referent is that to which a stretch of language refers in the world. Referential describes uses of language that achieve this, rather than simply referring to other language.

Relativism denies the existence of absolute values. Some endorse it because judgments are held to have no meaning in isolation while contexts may vary infinitely. In ancient Greek philosophy Protagoras (c. 490–410 B.C.) endorsed relativism, declaring that "Man is the measure of all things." In modern times the relativist Richard Rorty (1931–2007) preferred the term "ethnocentric" to denote that all truth is supposedly relative to our human and social point of view.

Semiotics means the study or science of signs or symbols, in contrast to semantics, which normally denotes the study of meanings. Ferdinand de Saussure (1857–1913) is associated with semiotics in Europe, just as C. S. Peirce (1839–1914) is in America. Roland Barthes (1915–80) extended the term, challenging any "natural" relation between the sign and the signified, and he and Jacques Derrida (1930–2004) placed the term in the context of postmodernism. Semiotics enters hermeneutics when we discuss such subjects as allegory, metaphor, signification, and communication.

Socio-pragmatic contextualism stands in contrast to socio-critical contextualism, which seeks to penetrate beneath contextual phenomena to find the underlying basis for them. The socio-pragmatic focuses simply of the *effect* of contextualism. These are represented respectively by Habermas and Rorty or Fish. Contextualism describes a collection of views in philosophy that emphasize the context in which an action, utterance, or expression occurs, and argues that, in some important respect, an action, utterance, or expression can only be understood relative to that context.

Speech acts (also known as performative utterances and illocutions) were identified by John L. Austin (1911–60) and developed by John Searle (b. 1932). The terms denote an utterance or stretch of language that does not merely say something but does something or performs an act in the saying of it. A promise, for example, does not merely say something but commits the speaker to perform or act on the promise. A pledge constitutes another example. Austin called making a promise a "commissive" because it committed the speaker to acting. These may also be termed illocutions. Illocutions perform an action *in* saying something; by contrast perlocutions perform an action *by* saying something. "By saying" indicates a causal force while "in saying" depends on illocutionary force alone.

Structuralism began with many influences, especially the binary contrasts suggested by Claude Lévy-Strauss (1908–2009). These were drawn from his kinship systems (or structures) in social anthropology, for example where "husband" drew its significance from its contrast with "wife" and "sister." Meanings of words depend on their *role within a system*, for example, in color words "red" differs from either "yellow" or "orange" depending on its system. Trier argued that words have meaning "only within a system." But since that time structuralism has taken numerous forms, including the "structural grammar" of Vladimir Propp, A. J. Greimas, and Gérard Genette in their theories of narrative. Propp identified thirty-one functions, such as hero and villain, helper and opponent, and so on. Eventually some degree of skepticism led to "post-structuralism."

Sub-codes often presuppose professional training or a level of competency among readers. They incorporate judgments that are learned and are therefore different from codes as such, which may be entirely conventional. Sub-codes may operate within a professional guild.

Typifications are borrowed from Max Weber in sociology to refer to typical social roles in historical reconstructions in hermeneutics, as defended especially by Emilio Betti. He argued that this assisted understanding in the context of intersubjective (see earlier) life.

Under-coded texts are those where the code is insufficiently explicit and gives rise to ambiguity.

Bibliography

Alter, Robert. *The Art of Biblical Narrative.* New York: Basic, 1981.

Apel, Karl-Otto. *Understanding and Explanation: A Transcendental-Pragmatic Perspective.* Massachusetts: MIT Press, 1985.

Aristotle. *Poetics.* London: Penguin, 1996.

Augustine. *Confessions.* Oxford: Oxford University Press, 1991.

Austin, John L. *How to Do Things with Words.* Oxford: Clarendon, 1962.

Bakhtin, Mikhail. *Problems of Dostoevsky's Poetics.* Minneapolis: Minnesota University, 1984.

Barfield, Owen. "Poetic Diction and Legal Fiction." In *The Importance of Language,* edited by Max Black, 51–71. Englewood Cliffs, NJ: Prentice-Hall, 1963.

Bauman, Zygmunt. *Hermeneutics and Social Science: Approaches to Understanding.* London: Hutchinson, 1978.

———. *Intimations of Postmodernity.* London: Routledge, 1992.

Berger, Peter, and Thomas Luckmann. *The Social Construction of Reality: A Treatise in the Sociology of Knowledge.* London: Penguin, 1966.

Bernstein, Richard J., ed. *Habermas and Modernity.* Cambridge: Polity, 1985.

Betti, Emilio. *Allgemeine Auslegungslehre als Methodik der Geisteswissenschaften.* Tübingen: Mohr, 1967.

———. *Zur Grundlegung einer allgemeinen Auslegungslehre.* 1955. Reprint, Tübingen: Mohr, 1988.

Black Max, ed. *The Importance of Language.* Englewood Cliffs, NJ: Prentice-Hall, 1963.

———. *Models and Metaphors.* Ithaca, NY: Cornell University Press, 1962.

Bultmann, Rudolf. "Is Exegesis without Presuppositions Possible?" In *Existence and Faith: Shorter Writings of Rudolf Bultmann,* 342–51. ET. London: Fontana, 1964.

———. "The Problem of Hermeneutics." In *Essays Philosophical and Theological,* 234–46. ET. London: SCM, 1955.

———. *Theology of the New Testament,* Vol. 1. ET. London: SCM, 1952.

———. *This World and Beyond: Marburg Sermons.* London: Lutterworth, 1960.

———. "What Does It Mean to Speak of God?" In *Faith and Understanding: Collected Essays*, 53–65. London: SCM, 1969.

Burtchaell, James T. *Catholic Theories of Biblical Inspiration since 1810: A Review and Critique.* Cambridge: Cambridge University Press, 1969.

Chatman, Seymour. *Story and Discourse: Narrative Structure in Fiction and Film.* Ithaca, NY: Cornell University Press, 1978.

Clark, Katrina, and Michael Holquist. *Mikhail Bakhtin.* Cambridge: Harvard University Press, 1984.

Crossan, John Dominic. *In Parables.* New York: Harper & Row, 1973.

Derrida, Jacques. "White Mythology: Metaphor in the Text of Philosophy." In *Margins of Philosophy*, 207–72. ET. London: Harvester, 1982.

Dilthey, Wilhelm. *Critique of Historical Reason.* ET. Chicago: Chicago University Press, 1978.

———. *Gesammelte Schriften.* Vols. 1–26. Göttingen: Vandenhoeck & Ruprecht, 1914–2005 (especially vols. 5 and 7 on hermeneutics).

———. "The Rise of Hermeneutics." *New Literary History* 3 (1972) 229–41.

Dobschütz, Ernst von. "Interpretation." In *The Encyclopaedia of Religion and Ethics*, edited by James Hastings, 7:390–95. Edinburgh: T. & T. Clark, 1914.

Dodd, Charles H. *The Parables of the Kingdom.* London: Nisbet, 1935.

Ebeling, Gerhard. *Word and Faith.* ET. London: SCM, 1963.

Eco, Umberto. *The Role of the Reader: Explorations in the Theory of the Semiotics of Texts.* London: Hutchinson, 1981.

———. *Semiotics and the Philosophy of Language.* London; MacMillan, 1984.

———. *A Theory of Semiotics.* Bloomington, IN: Indiana University Press, 1976.

Fish, Stanley. *Doing What Comes Naturally: Change, Rhetoric, and the Practice of Theory in Literary and Legal Studies.* Oxford: Clarendon, 1989.

———. *Is There a Text in This Class? The Authority of Interpretive Communities.* Cambridge: Cambridge University Press, 1980.

Frye, Northrop. *The Great Code: The Bible and Literature.* New York: Harcourt Bruce Jovanovich, 1982.

Fuchs, Ernst. *Hermeneutik.* Tübingen: Mohr, 1970.

———. "The New Testament and the Hermeneutical Problem." In *New Frontiers in Theology: The New Hermeneutic*, edited by James Robinson and John Cobb, 111–46. New York: Harper & Row, 1964.

———. *Studies of the Historical Jesus.* ET. London: SCM, 1964.

Funk, Robert W. *Language, Hermeneutic and Word of God.* New York: Harper & Row, 1966.

———. *Parables and Presence: Forms of the New Testament Tradition.* Philadelphia: Fortress, 1982.

Gadamer, Hans-Georg. *Philosophical Hermeneutics.* ET. Berkeley: University of California Press, 1976.

———. *Truth and Method.* 2nd ed. ET. London: Sheed and Ward, 1989.

Genette, Gérard. *Narrative Discourse.* ET. Ithaca, NY: Cornell University Press, 1980.

Genisas, Saulus. *The Origin of the Horizon in Husserl's Phenomenology*. Munich: Springer, 2012.

Haber, Honi Fern. *Beyond Postmodern Politics: Lyotard, Rorty, Foucault*. London: Routledge, 1994.

Habermas, Jürgen., "The Hermeneutic Claim to Universality." In *Contemporary Hermeneutics: Hermeneutics as Method, Philosophy, and Critique*, edited by Josef Bleicher, 181–211. London: Routledge, 1980.

―――. *Knowledge and Human Interests*. ET. London: Heinemann, 1978.

―――. *The Theory of Communicative Action: The Critique of Functionalist Reason*. 2 vols. ET. Cambridge: Polity, 1984 and 1987.

Hahn, Lewis E., ed. *The Philosophy of Hans-Georg Gadamer*. La Salle, IL: Open Court, 1997.

Hart, H. L. A. "The Ascription of Responsibility and Rights." *Proceedings of the Aristotelian Society* 49 (1948) 171–94.

Heidegger, Martin. *Being and Time*. ET. Oxford: Blackwell, 1962.

Hesse, Mary. *Models and Analogies in Science*. London: Sheed & Ward, 1963.

Hodges, H. A. *The Philosophy of Wilhelm Dilthey*. London: Routledge, 1952.

Husserl, Edmund. *Cartesian Meditations: An Introduction to Phenomenology*. New York: Springer, 1929.

Ihde, Don. *Hermeneutic Phenomenology: The Philosophy of Paul Ricoeur*. Evanston, IL: Northwestern, 1971.

Jeremias, Joachim. *The Parables of Jesus*. Rev. ed. ET. London: SCM, 1963.

Jones, Geraint Vaughan. *The Art and Truth of the Parables: A Study in Their Literary Form and Modern Interpretation*. London: SPCK, 1964.

Jülicher, Adolf. *Die Gleichnisreden Jesu*. 2 vols. Tübingen: Mohr, 1888.

Jung, Carl Gustav. *Man and His Symbols*. New York: Doubleday, 1971.

Jüngel, Eberhard. *Theological Essays*. Edinburgh: T. & T. Clark, 1989.

Kierkegaard, Søren. *Fear and Trembling: Dialectical Lyric by Johannes de Silentio*. ET. London: Penguin, 1985.

―――. *Purity of Heart Is to Will One Thing*. ET. London: Collins/Fontana, 1961.

Kissinger, Warren S. *The Parables of Jesus: A History of Interpretation and Bibliography*. London: Scarecrow, 1979.

Klemm, David E. *The Hermeneutical Theory of Paul Ricoeur*. Lewisburg, PA: Bucknell University Press, 1983.

Lakoff, George, and Mark Johnson. *Metaphors We Live By*. 1980. Reprint, Chicago: Chicago University Press, 2003.

Lewis, C. S. "Bluspels and Flanansferes." In *The Importance of Language*, edited by Max Black, 36–50. Englewood Cliffs, NJ: Prentice-Hall, 1962.

Linnemann, Eta. *The Parables of Jesus*. ET. London: SPCK, 1966.

Lonergan, Bernard. *Insight: A Study of Human Understanding*. New York: Harper & Row, 1978.

Longman, Tremper. *Literary Approaches to Biblical Interpretation*. Grand Rapids: Academie, 1987.

BIBLIOGRAPHY

Lyotard, Jean-François. *The Postmodern Condition*. ET. Manchester: Manchester University Press, 1984.

——. *The Postmodern Explained to Children: Correspondence 1982–85*. ET. London: Turnaround, 1992.

Makreel, Rudolf A., and F. Rodi, eds. *Wilhelm Dilthey: Selected Works*. Vol. 1. Princeton: Princeton University Press, 1969.

Mannheim, Karl. *Ideology and Utopia: Introduction to the Sociology of Knowledge*. London: Routledge, 1960.

Marx, Karl, and Friedrich Engels. *Über Kunst und Literatur*. 2 vols. Berlin: Dietz, 1967–68.

Morgan, Robert, with John Barton. *Biblical Interpretation*. Oxford: Oxford University Press, 1988.

Morson Gary S., and Caryl Emerson. *Mikhail Bakhtin: Creation of a Prosaics*. Stanford: Standford University Press, 1990.

Mueller-Vollmer, Kurt, ed. *The Hermeneutics Reader: Texts of the German Tradition from the Enlightenment to the Present*. Oxford: Blackwell/ Continuum, 1985.

Nietzsche, Friedrich. *On Truth and Lies in a Nonmoral Sense*. 1873. ET. London: Penguin, 1990.

Palmer, Richard E. *Hermeneutics: Interpretation Theory in Schleiermacher, Dilthey, Heidegger, and Gadamer*. Evanston, IL: Northwestern University Press, 1969.

Pannenberg, Wolfhart. *Theology and the Philosophy of Science*. ET. Philadelphia: Westminster, 1976.

Paul, Ian. "Metaphor." In *Dictionary for Theological Interpretation of the Bible*, edited by K. J. Vanhoozer, 507–10. London: SPCK, 2005.

Pellauer, David. *Ricoeur: A Guide for the Perplexed*. London: Continuum, 2007.

Peterson, Norman. "The Reader in the Gospel." *Neotestamentica* 18 (1984) 38–51.

Porter, Stanley E., and Matthew R. Malcolm, eds. *Horizons in Hermeneutics*. Grand Rapids: Eerdmans, 2013.

Ramsey, Ian T. *Models and Mystery*. London: Oxford University Press, 1964.

Ray, William. *Literary Meaning: from Phenomenology to Deconstruction*. Oxford: Blackwell, 1984.

Readings, Bil. *Introducing Lyotard: Art and Politics*. London: Routledge, 1991.

Ricoeur, Paul. *The Conflict of Interpretations: Essays in Hermeneutics*. Evanston, IL: Northwestern University Press, 1974.

——. *Essays in Biblical Interpretation*. Edited with an introduction by Lewis S. Mudge. ET. Minneapolis: Fortress, 1980.

——. "Existence and Hermeneutics." In *The Conflict of Interpretations*, 3–24. Evanston, IL: Northwestern University Press, 1974.

——. *Fallible Man*. ET. New York: Fordham University Press, 1985.

——. *Figuring the Sacred: Religion, Narrative, and Imagination*. ET. Minneapolis: Fortress, 1995.

———. *Freedom and Nature.* ET. Evanston, IL: Northwestern University Press, 1966

———. *Freud and Philosophy: An Essay on Interpretation.* ET. New Haven: Yale University Press, 1970.

———. *From Text to Action: Essays in Hermeneutics.* ET. London: Continuum, 1991.

———. *Hermeneutics and the Human Sciences: Essays on Language, Action and Interpretation.* ET. Cambridge: Cambridge University Press, 1981.

———. "Intellectual Autobiography." In *The Philosophy of Paul Ricoeur,* edited by Lewis Edwin Hahn, 3–53. Chicago: Open Court, 1995.

———. *Interpretation Theory: Discourse and Surplus of Meaning.* Fort Worth, TX: Texas Christian University Press, 1976.

———. "Metaphor and Symbol." In *Interpretation Theory: Discourse and the Surplus of Meaning,* 45–70. Fort Worth, TX: Texas Christian University Press, 1976.

———. "The Narrative Form." *Semeia* 4 (1975) 37–73.

———. "The Nuptial Metaphor." In Ricoeur and LaCocque, *Thinking Biblically,* 265–303. Chicago: Chicago University Press, 1998.

———. *Oneself as Another.* ET. Chicago: Chicago University Press, 1992.

———. "Preface to Bultmann." In Ricoeur, *Essays in Biblical Interpretation,* edited by Lewis Mudge, 49–72. ET. Minneapolis: Fortress, 1980.

———. *The Rule of Metaphor: Multi-disciplinary Studies of the Creation of Meaning in Language.* ET. London: Routledge, 1978

———. *The Symbolism of Evil.* ET. Boston: Beacon, 1969.

———. *Time and Narrative.* 3 vols. ET. Chicago: University Press, 1984, 1985, and 1988.

———. "Toward a Hermeneutic of the Idea of Revelation." In *Essays on Biblical Interpretation,* edited by Lewis Mudge, 73–118. Minneapolis: Fortress, 1980.

Ricoeur, Paul, and André LaCocque. *Thinking Biblically: Exegetical and Hermeneutical Studies.* Chicago: Chicago University Press, 1998.

Rickman, H. P., ed. *Wilhelm Dilthey: Selected Writings.* Cambridge: Cambridge University Press, 1976.

Robinson, James M. "Hermeneutic Since Barth." In *New Frontiers in Theology: vol. 2. The New Hermeneutic,* edited by James M. Robinson and John B. Cobb, 1–77. New York: Harper & Row, 1964.

Rogers, Jack, and Donald McKim. *The Authority and Inspiration of the Bible: A Historical Approach.* Grand Rapids: Eerdmans, 1979.

Rollins, Wayne G. *Jung and the Bible.* Atlanta: John Knox, 1983.

Rorty, Richard. *The Consequences of Pragmatism.* Minnesota: University of Minnesota Press, 1982.

———. *Contingency, Irony, and Solidarity.* Cambridge: Cambridge University Press, 1989.

———. *Objectivism, Relativism, and Truth.* Cambridge: Cambridge University Press, 1991.

———. *Philosophy and the Mirror of Nature*. Princeton: Princeton University Press, 1979.

———. *Philosophy as Cultural Politics*. Cambridge: Cambridge University Press, 2007.

———. *Truth and Progress: Philosophical Papers 3*. Cambridge: Cambridge University Press, 1999.

Schleiermacher, Friedrich. *Hermeneutics: The Handwritten Manuscripts*. Edited by H. Kimmerle. ET. Missoula, MT: Scholars, 1977.

Searle, John R., *Intentionality. An Essay in the Philosophy of Mind*. Cambridge: Cambridge University Press, 1983.

Soskice, Janet Martin. *Metaphor and Religious Language*. Oxford: Clarendon, 1985.

Stroup, George. *The Promise of Narrative Theology*. London: SCM, 1984.

Thiselton, Anthony C. *Can the Bible Mean Whatever We Want It to Mean?* Chester, UK: Chester Academic Press, Inaugural Lecture, 2005.

———. *New Horizons in Hermeneutics*. London: HarperCollins, 1992. (2nd ed., Grand Rapids: Zondervan, 2012.)

———. *The Power of Pictures in Christian Thought: The Use and Abuse of Images in the Bible and Theology*. London: SPCK, 2018.

———. "Reception History, H. R. Jauss, and the Formative Power of Scripture." *Scottish Journal of Theology* 65 (2012) 289–308.

———. *Thiselton on Hermeneutics: The Collected Works and New Essays of Anthony Thiselton*. Aldershot, UK: Ashgate, 2006.

———. *The Two Horizons: New Testament Hermeneutics and Philosophical Description*. Exeter, UK: Paternoster, 1980.

Tillich, Paul. *Dynamics of Faith*. London: Allen & Unwin, 1957.

———. "The Religious Symbol." In *Religious Experience and Truth*, edited by Sydney Hook, 3–11. Edinburgh: Oliver and Boyd, 1961.

———. *The Shaking of the Foundations*. London: SCM, 1962.

———. *Systematic Theology*. 3 vols. London: Nisbet, 1957–64.

Vanhoozer, Kevin J. *Biblical Narrative in the Philosophy of Paul Ricoeur: A Study in Hermeneutics and Theology*. Cambridge: Cambridge University Press, 1990.

Via, Dan Otto. *The Parables: Their Literary and Existential Dimension*. Philadelphia: Fortress, 1967.

Wheelwright, Philip. *The Burning Fountain: A Study in the Language of Symbolism*. Tulamore, Ireland: Midland, 1954.

———. *Metaphor and Reality*. Bloomington, IN: Indiana University, 1962.

White, Stephen. *The Recent Work of Jürgen Habermas: Reason, Justice, and Modernity*. Cambridge: Cambridge University Press, 1988.

Wilder, Amos. *Early Christian Rhetoric*. London: SCM, 1964.

Wink, Walter. *The Bible in Human Transformation: Toward a New Paradigm for Biblical Study*. Philadelphia: Fortress, 1973.

Wittgenstein, Ludwig. *Philosophical Investigations*. 3rd ed. Oxford: Blackwell, 1967.

————. *Zettel*. German and English. Oxford: Blackwell, 1967.

Wolterstorff, Nicholas. *Works and Worlds of Art*. Oxford: Clarendon, 1980.

Woodbridge, John D. *Biblical Inspiration and Authority: A Critique of the Rogers/McKim Proposal*. Grand Rapids: Zondervan, 1982.

Index of Principal
Biblical References

INDEX OF PRINCIPAL BIBLICAL REFERENCES

Index of Subjects

Index of Names

Made in the USA
Columbia, SC
19 January 2024

30694407R00086